SHADOWS IN DEFERMENT

Birgit Bunzel Linder

Supported by

The Hong Kong Arts Development Council fully supports freedom of artistic expression. The views and opinions expressed in this project do not represent the stand of the Council.

SHADOWS IN DEFERMENT won the International Proverse Prize 2012. A representative collection of free verse from a life of rich cultural encounters, it cannot be read at one sitting but must be savoured over time, and more than once, if justice is to be done to the ideas and the means by which they are expressed. Attempts at self-identification are matched by the permanent impressions made by new cultures and social contexts. Linguistic and spiritual displacement are articulated, while the poet also offers a sense of and search for a common humanity. Striking images created by the poet provide an extra dimension.

BIRGIT BUNZEL LINDER was born and raised in Oberhausen, an industrial city in the Ruhr Valley. She left Germany in the 1980s, and has since lived in Taiwan, China, America, and now lives in Hong Kong. She teaches Chinese and Comparative Literary Studies at the City University of Hong Kong. Her life has been marked by frequent moves and many travels, and by inscriptions from different places, cultures, and people, which also reveal themselves in her first collection of poetry, *Shadows in Deferment*. Birgit Linder has previously published poems in *Mad Poets Review, Clockwise Cat, Kavya Bharati, Cerebration, International Literary Quarterly,* and *Asian Cha*. Besides writing, she likes painting, reading, and photography.

SHADOWS IN DEFERMENT

Birgit Bunzel Linder

Proverse Hong Kong

Shadows in Deferment
by Birgit Bunzel Linder.
2nd pbk edition published in Hong Kong by Proverse Hong Kong,
August 2016
Copyright © Proverse Hong Kong, August 2016.
ISBN: 978-988-8228-59-1
Available from https://createspace.com/6412749

1st published in Hong Kong by Proverse Hong Kong, November 2013.
Copyright © Proverse Hong Kong, June 2012, November 2013.
ISBN 978-988-8227-16-7

Enquiries: Proverse Hong Kong, P.O. Box 259, Tung Chung Post Office,
Tung Chung, Lantau Island, NT, Hong Kong SAR, China.
E-mail: proverse@netvigator.com
Web site: www.proversepublishing.com

The right of Birgit Bunzel Linder to be identified as the author of this
work has been asserted by her
in accordance with the Copyright, Designs and Patents Act 1988.

Cover image by and with kind permission of Birgit Bunzel Linder.
Page design by Proverse Hong Kong.
Images by Birgit Bunzel Linder.

All rights reserved. No part of this publication may be reproduced, stored in a retrieval system, or transmitted, in any form or by any means, electronic, mechanical, photocopying, recording or otherwise, without the prior written permission of the publisher or publisher and author. The book is sold subject to the condition that it shall not, by way of trade or otherwise, be lent, re-sold, hired out or otherwise circulated without the publisher's prior written consent in any form of binding or cover other than that in which it is published and without a similar condition including this condition being imposed on the subsequent owner or purchaser. Please contact Proverse Hong Kong in writing, to request any and all permissions (including but not restricted to republishing, inclusion in anthologies, translation, reading, performance and use as set pieces in examinations and festivals).

British Library Cataloguing in Publication Data.
A catalogue record for this book is available from the British Library.

Previous publication acknowledgements

Poems

'Fickle Soul in Suzhou'. *Cerebration* 1 & 2, 2007/2008.
'Ghosts of a Generation,' 'You and I'. *Clockwise Cat* 4 (September 2007).
'How Hong Kong Was Made'. *Asian Cha* 17 (July 2012).
'New Year in Precipitous Valley Village'. (Now retitled, 'New Year in Dougou Village'.) *Mad Poets Review* 18: 99, 2003.
'Rumi, or My Heart is a Vagabond', 'Simply Darwish: Black Rain Storm', 'Some Observations at a Coffee Shop in Suzhou'. *International Literary Quarterly* (UK) 15 (May 2011).
'India'. *Kavya Bharati: A Review of Indian Poetry 19: 59*, 2007.

Image

'An Urban Friend'. *Asian Cha* 18 (September 2012). (*Shadows in Deferment*, p. 78.)

Shadows in Deferment

Contents

I SHADOWS/REFLECTIONS

I, Too, Sing This Country	14
Water at Night	15
Shadow	17
Animus Revertendi	19
All Saints' Day	20
Mother	22
King of Other People	23
Man on the Moon	25
Birds of Paradise Flee Toward East	26
The Dis/Quiet of Exile	27
Sunday Afternoon	28
The Narrow Path	30
late autumn	31
A Canary in the Coalmines	32

II COINCIDENCES

rain stories	35
Twelve Topknots in Taipo	36
Samurai Dreamers	38
Sister Butterfly	39
Sneeze	40
An Evening at the Ocean	41
like lashes	42
Fickle Soul in Suzhou	43
Some Observations at a Coffee Shop in Suzhou	45
the thought: he disappeared	47
lotus	48
The Y Not Taken	49
Homeless	50

III BETWEEN PEOPLE

A Seaside Tree	53
A Quiet Life	54
Salaam	56
Song of White Hair	57
Still Missing You	58
Sudden Theft	60
A Grave Digger in Exile	61
Buried Alive	62
Destiny	63
An Ode to Dulin Figs	64
God's Intentions	65
Do Not Count Our Days	66
Loneliness	67
Broken in the Morning	68
At a Loss	69
A Cake, a Stew, and a Thousand Smiles	70
Winter Coat	72
Simply Kafka: Pinky Swear!	75
Sharpshooting Memories	74
Between People	75
Simply Darwish: In the End	76

IV GHOSTS OF A GENERATION

Ghosts of a Generation	79
You and I	80
The Fancy Maoist Tienu at the Monument of the People	82
Wounded Soldier	84
A Mother-Tongue in Exile	86
Hu-Manity	88
White Sparrow	89
An Urban Home	91

Swallows and Spirits	93
A Man From the Walled City	95
The Once Red Scholar or June the Third	96
Cloud Dreams	97
A UN Diplomat in a Hong Kong Jewelry Store	98
just one word	100
A Portrait in the Old Webbed Attic	101
The Gods are in a Messy Mood	102

V   RAVING SOULS

A Raving Soul	105
A Poet's Demons	107
Rumi, or My Heart is a Vagabond	109
Gatekeeper	111
Osmanthus of Despair	113
Hawk of Depression	114
Li Yu, Waley, and I	115
Yellow Like Poems, Like Prose	116
What Wittgenstein Said	118
White Flag	119
Black Crows	120
Meridians of the Soul	121
At Night We Drink	122
A Swinger of Moods	123
Echo Mountain	124

VI   IN THIS WORLD

Simply Darwish: Black Rain Storm	127
Simply Darwish: Common Humanity	129
Peace	131
The People's Daily	133
Spies of Sorrow Come in Battalions	134
Actuality	135
Simply Kafka: The Rope	136

First Day of Winter	137
Writing After Dinner in Tamil Nadu	138
To Everycity Turn, Turn, Turn	139
How Hong Kong Was Made	140
I Still Think That!	141
Xanthippe	142
Life of a Beetle	144
A Progressive Ant	145
Narrow Minded	146
Retreat	147
Nachtraeglichkeit	148
Fairy Whispers	150

VII PLACES

India	153
Day of the Strange Tide	154
Morning Has Broken	155
northern moor	156
Imperial City	157
Great Wall Cocoon	158
Fall in Nancun	159
Poughkeepsie Valley	161
Tartan	162
Over Nebraska	163
Askance Glance Over New England	164
Ruhrpott Song	165
Splendour of the Visayas	166
In the Bamboo Grove	167
New Year in Dougou Village	168

VIII IN SHORT

The Habit of Turning Into a Shadow	171
Simply Kafka: The Cage	171
Saturday Morning	172

You	172
August Rain in Hong Kong	173
Phone Call	173
Anger	174
The Rooster	174
Bygone	175
Your Tenderness	175
Comfort	176
The Way Things Are	176
Life	176
Advance Review: The Icing on the Cage by Simon Patton	177
Advance Review: Defamiliarising Our Daily Bread by Stuart Christie	180
The Publishers	187
The International Proverse Prize for Unpublished Book-Length Fiction, Non-Fiction or Poetry	188
The International Proverse Poetry Prize (Single Poems)	189
Poetry Published by Proverse	190

SHADOWS / REFLECTIONS

I, Too, Sing This Country

It wakes me every hour—
On a strict schedule
That moves to a regular rhythm,
Ca-dence, ca-dence, ca-dence.
It rumbles on until I fall asleep again,
And I dream of meters,
Of dissonances and sudden
Enjambments, and I am
Attacked by iambic feet,
Strangled by trochaic lines,
And sentenced to rattle on and on
In this long-distance train of thought,
And Whitman is the captain....
I toss and turn from grass to stars
And back to myself.
I cannot sleep for all I hear is
Germany singing...
America singing...
China singing...
Finally, when the sun almost rises
And a nation finds its caesura,
I nod off and I dream
Of raisins, Niemandsrosen, and wild geese
Until the train is once more deferred:
A darkish man pulls the stops and shouts,
"Listen up folks! I, too, sing this place!"
And he sings a weary blues
That assumes what I assume
And then he moves the train
Into cadences again.

Water at Night

In the middle of every night,
the moon's noise wakes me.
I hear water everywhere.

Water that whispers in capillaries.
Water that hides under cracks.
Water white with soap.
Water quiet from coal.
Water that drips into the aquarium.
Water that leaps from the roof.
Water that cascades down the stairs.
Water that rushes over the road.

Water always goes the path of least resistance.
Water always finds a way.

Water has ways to flow in places far away.
One can cross the waters to America.
Or to the Cape of Good Hope.
Water scuttles ice down the Red River.
Water mollifies the leatherbacks in Nicobar.
Water carries you through monsoon jungles,
and eases you down to warlorn submarines.

Half asleep I search for the white bucket,
like every night,
fill it with warm water.
Water draws women to the well,
where it changes from dark to light.
I reach for my father's weary feet
that have come in from the dusty road,
like every night,
to wash his tiredness away.
Water washes away guilt.

But his chair is empty.
The pillow has fallen
onto the exhausted rug.
Water is a carpet to the faithful.
Water is always more than itself.

Or less, the Mariner says.
Yes, I envy the ocean's generosity,
that lets its fish swim freely.
I pour the water into the fish tank.
It changes from dark to light.
I feel water everywhere.
It is rising to my eyes.
Maybe I, too, have lived too long
where I can be reached.*

---

* Rumi

Schatten   Shadow   影子

Ich sehe dir beim Rasieren zu.
    I watch you shave.
        我看你
Vor dem Spiegel.
    In front of the mirror.
        在镜前刮脸.
Ich erzähle dir von meinem Vater:
    I tell you about my father:
        我和你说到我父亲:
Sein Trinken.
    His drinking.
        他酗酒.
Sein kriegsversehrtes Bein.
    His war-torn leg.
        他战伤的腿.
Seine Schutzlosigkeit.
    His defenselessness.
        他毫无戒备.
Seine vielen Verluste.
    His many losses.
        他的累累败绩.
Und verschwiegene Siege.
    And untold victories.
        以及从未与人言的胜利.

我不是你的父亲.
    I am not your father.
        Ich bin nicht dein Vater.
你语气恼怒.
    You say, annoyed.
        Sagst du irritiert.
我并未见过父亲刮脸.
    I never watched him shave.

        Ich habe ihm nie beim Rasieren zugesehen.
我辩白说.
    I defend myself.
        Verteidige ich mich.
Yet I know:
    但我知道:
        Aber ich weiss:
I will never be a woman
    我绝不会是一个
        Ich werde niemals eine Frau sein
Without shadow.
    没有影子的女人.
        ohne Schatten.

Animus Revertendi

I read it like wine
I recite it like dance
I pirouette around stanzas
I exhale caesurae

I adopt paratactics
I enjamb my breath
I metaphorse lines
I alliterate your tears

I perform without rhyme
I syncopate our heartbeats
I entitle myself
I become a poem

I stamp it on the wings of a swallow
And let it disperse above reach
I scratch it onto the scutes of turtles
And send it out into the sea

I dispatch it into fallen leaves
So something old can stay
I hurl it out of my blazing heart
To brand it for public display

All Saints' Day

We prepare for the cemetery when
dew has turned to rain to frost to hail.
At season's infancy, they say.
Jittery trees line our cobbled streets,
standing bare and reaching high.
The roots hold on to the hardened soil,
afraid to lose their ground.

In the morning we bring out our sleep,
wrapped in knit sweaters.
We exhale our souls on the way to school;
winter makes us silent.
In the evening jinni lurk at every corner,
until we confine them to red candles on the graves.

We polish the marble with our gloves,
wander by soldiers' crosses that look
forlorn and tired, candles
flickering like orphans.
We wait in solemn silence and count
the flames that have died so far.

Tonight the dead come alive.
But you and I die a little further.
Grown-ups groom shifty memories.
The dead don't mind the gossip
that sweeps from grave to grave.

Every year we search for better secrets.
Although we know their stories.
Tonight, we all are saints, they say.
While they whisper revelations,
we tug on their coats and ask,
"When does death begin?"
"When the heart begins to beat
dutifully," Mother says.

On the way home, our breath hangs
in the air like budding ghosts.
The cobble stones put demons in our way.
Black trees climb out of their leaves,
whip unseen ghouls and ghosts.
Our hearts beat, beat, beat. Beat wildly.

And so we go to sleep in peace,
knowing that death is far off and preoccupied
with saints and sinners
from the past and the present.

Mother

So much more than you
died that day when I
laboured with this life.
Now the child is tall,
plucks the first ripe fruit
off the youthful tree
on your pregnant grave.
While he chews his pear,
full of reverence,
I hold a belly
full of barbed thoughts.

King of Other People

Six years. She is. She wakes.
A ray of sunshine polishes
the golden inscription on her altar.
Where Jesus hangs.
Her Jesus. Her saviour. INRI.
Whose King is he?
She opens it. The Catholic catechism.
To the legend of Robin Redbreast
whose chest was dyed crimson
with a drop of sacrificial blood.
The miracle. Of death.

Six years. She is. She freezes.
Sits on the radiator to watch
an autumn morning. Very early.
Leaves play catch. Fog slows them down.
There is Ruby, the robin. Perched.
On the old peach tree.
Bird and peach leaves both have red spots.

But then,
with the suddenness of a November gust,
the branches bow toward the grass.
The bird is scared off
the clothesline
usually used
for their largest sheets.
She has never seen the tree
bow so wildly,
throwing the last of fall to the ground.
Just like Papa yesterday
at Mama's funeral.

She averts her puzzled look
to the crucifix. INRI. Jesus,
King of Other People.

Man on the Moon

When Mr Armstrong stepped
onto the moon, it was 1969.
That was also the year
when we mastered our deafness.
The year before, we still listened:
When she yelled,
Maria Callas sang to us.
When she cried,
we heard raindrops drip.
When she smashed cups and plates,
we heard wind chimes jingle.
But in 1969, when I asked,
"Where were you last night?"
You laughed and said, "I heard
nothing." And I,
when your door closed behind him,
was deaf to your sobs.
In the morning,
you did not ask me where I was.
But we laughed together
when we watched the moon
being invaded by mankind.

Birds of Paradise Flee Toward East

Two birds of paradise flee toward east,
tweet Upanishads, look
outward, inward, upward.
They laugh, and they eat, they drink.
They fly into clouds of Shanti peace,
peck at the order of the metallic sky.
They have no empty branch to settle on,
but spread their wings over orchards
of our blooming apocalypse.
They throw shadows into the e-t-h-e-r-i-z-e-d sky.
They listen to Nerval talk to tables and chairs.

They set out from the western windowsill
of the prophet who croons prophecies,
and land on the eastern balcony
of the dervish who whirls with joy.
They flee from the master tweetative
to learn to sing hybrid songs of peace.

When the birds of paradise come to you,
don't disregard the greatest gift.
They land on one shoulder each
and have become yours.
Why still climb up on the rooftop
and expose them?
Wrap them up instead
in your warm winter skin.

The Dis/Quiet of Exile

Cedar Creek, 5:07am.
The first snow in northern reserves
weighs our fall into lone confinement.
A left boot suffocates at 5:40am.
A white glowworm plague
invades the long vacant house.

This silence, the disquiet of exile.

Into the icy breath of abandon,
the phone rings shrill, at 5:43am.
In the hollow emptiness,
it swells in waves toward the window,
sequesters through the glass,
and sinks into the snow like the moon,
sinks into the paling hills.
Twelve times, until the connection is cut.

Then the songs of the trees sink, too,
and follow the trails of the fox
until the calm bows heavy again,
like the long forgotten apple tree
carrying fruit of stone.

I wake up and hold your hand,
still warm with your own dreams.

Sunday Afternoon

Empty houses with closed blinds
in the Dordogne, on a summer Sunday:
Walls of cognac, doors of bordeaux.
Doves have tucked in their beaks.
The dusty Silence, the Loneliness,
as though it were in the Ruhr Valley:
Where the house is a cold white.

Loneliness is more voluminous on Sundays,
our Holy Day of Sleep.
Our Silence hangs beat
by a church tower bell
that sounds with hourly restraint.
The train approaches her watchfully,
but then hurries by after all.

Even the storm cancels its coming,
offended by the blue breath of the priests.
The birds have sold their songs,
they sit in the trees and stare
into our Silence that
the most pointed talons cannot pierce.

Over the asphalt, skirts of glass hover
and white incense spirits polter mutely.
Sunday, Holy Day of Sleepers.

The only ones who don't honour it
are the doves of doom on our roof.
They know what lies beneath
the Silence in this house.
They know our children still are
amateurs of tragedy.
In mocking cadence they coo:
Peace be with you, with you!

The Narrow Path

When you shelter me,
I move mountains.
Far from you,
I only shift sand.
An unbound heart harbours
three great virtues:
distance, purity, non-interference,
until it is weighed down
to an earth where
the path back is the narrow path.

late autumn

titmice and sparrows flock for food at dusk
farewells hang in the air like lanterns

hoarfrost weaves over black bark
cracks quilt the quiet lake

a flock of crows pace the underbrush
watching souls rise in rime fog

the wind sweeps the trees clean
leaves sink heavy with experience

saluting all that is fallen and free
knowing that all has begun

long before fever rises out of dew, long
before wisdom summons back the hawk

A Canary in the Coalmines

From this mid-autumn moon
the weaving maid throws
threads of golden sheen;
From the serene copper plate
with specks of silhouettes,
gazing from a dark sea,
like a canary
in the coalmines,
at hazy eyes,
a mellow glow.
This annum mirabilis
is all the same.
And so am I.
Yet only one of us
seems truly sad.
I wander in your white dust.
Children of violence.
Children of abuse.
Children of life gone askew.
Compared to the moon's witness
on this quaking earth,
my imprints are faint,
like the sooty shadow
of the dust fly
my brother carelessly flicked off
my starched white blouse.

COINCIDENCES

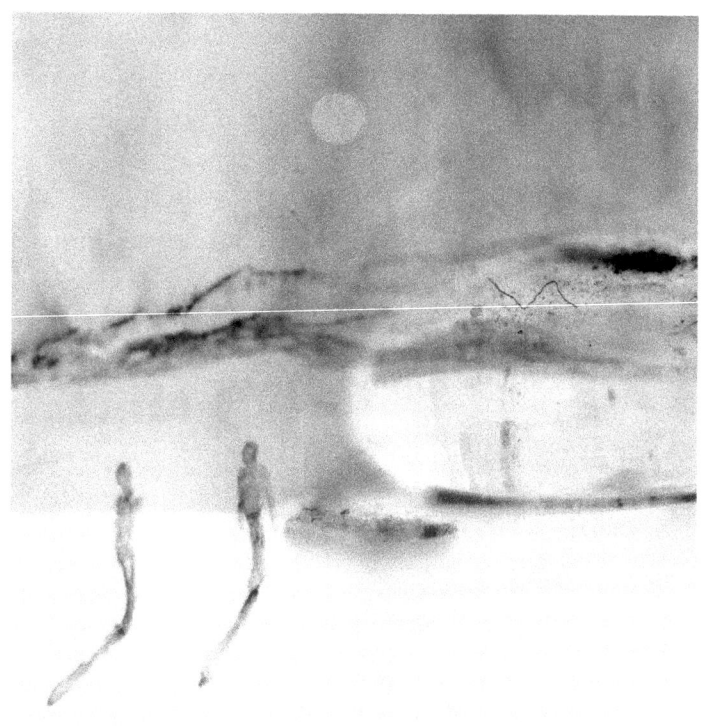

Shadows in Deferment

rain stories

rain falls into rivulets
each drop filled with a story
pushing down the wind
the swifts secure their homes
the wall leans on the ladder
far away horses stand
crossed by fences
shadows shrink into your skin
and darken your eyes
i lean over to you
the rain lights up your hair
i fall into your gaze and
lie down next to you
run out of words

Twelve Topknots in Taipo

Twelve Taoist novices
walk along the hillside road.

Twelve topknots popping up and down
like black beans in hot oil.

At the steep wayside,
bells suddenly toll.

Magically, three cell phones
fly out of three pockets.

Their chatter pitter-patters
across the street.

One hisses open
a bottle of coke.

Two tease the monkey
that came to beg for food.

They laugh, they point, they prattle,
and they re-adjust their black boot strings.

When one falls over,
the rest burst into delight.

When the master turns and calls
from fifty meters ahead,

magically, their phones disappear,
they reseal the bottle,

give alms to the ape,
and walk on,

heads bowed,
as though not at ease!

Samurai Dreamers

Three youths in black t-shirts
with badass razor shags
and shorts like sailor bags,

walk along the village road
under three umbrellas,
twirling G2000 fellas,

one medium,
one tall,
one small.

When the clouds run out of steam,
umbrellas suddenly swing
into samurai swords,

whipping the wet air
with ecstatic dare,
twisting in juvenile bliss.

When three girls call
across from University Hall,
they stand at attention.

Sheathing their swords with haste,
yet with chivalrous pace,
they cross the glistening road:

With heads carried tall,
as though not missing at all
those fancy boyhood dreams.

Sister Butterfly*

One yellow butterfly
got tired of hiding
in the fragrant ylang ylang tree.

She stretched her wings
and left her sister
to land on my nose, you see.

She looked right
into my left eye,
and she declared with glee:

"I just moved the world!"

"But, Colias Crocea," I say with dismay,
"your flapping wings
have changed nothing for me!"

"But, Homo Non-So-Sapiens," she replies,
"You just talked to a butterfly
from an ylang ylang tree!"

---

* A traditional Philippine tale speaks of two butterfly sisters—one green, one yellow—who are sheltered by the ylang ylang tree and, in return, the sisters gave the tree its famous aroma.

Sneeze

Your words and gestures pitter patter
onto my soul
like the almost frozen rain of Kayaderosseras.
Your subtleties turn into snow inching
up on my heart in silence—
white, innocent, pure,
silent and steady,
abidingly cold.
The melting power of blood
germinates into shivers and chills,
until all the flurry of activity
is summed up in a sneeze.
 "Gesundheit," says he
and hugs away the left-over frost.

I leave you that day
with the beautiful thought,
with the sad thought,
that you are
just a man.

An Evening at the Ocean

Birds are beaded straight on the wire
They gaze into the brewing sky
Dragonflies dangle in the air
Above shadows that fall into feeble forms

    I fill the shells with bread
        I grow a mountain out of a wave
        I sing a hymn to the copper moon

A loon cries at the borders of the night
With feathers as ruffled as memories
Stars spark fires behind blue brocade
And turn dry rocks into whispering stones

    I fill the shells with seeds
        I dispatch a ship into my heart
        I play a tune on my reed harp

The sooty tern floats wide awake
Across the mellow drowsy sea
Cattail guard the silver sand
That shapes into crescents with the wind

    I fill the shells with wine
        I wrap a turtle around my heart
        I set it free to roam in the dunes

like lashes

around the stirring sea polished shards gather.
rootless trees throw their rootless leaves
on the sand that grows into the banks.
the wind rearranges their path.
the cries of sea gulls are lost in the air.
some battered branches reach for the sky
where the sky touches the land.
above, the air wells up in domes.
i still see the sunset wave
from its golden throne.
a royal tern sits on the old lattice fence,
in a moment of silence.
quietly, quieter, it begins to sing
to its own quiet shadow.
a white feather lies entwined in wet foliage,
submerged like lashes in tears.
it was only just caught
in the lake's tossed chiffon
and i, alone in this mirror world,
think of the time
when i would have set it free.

Fickle Soul in Suzhou

In Hanshan Temple
tranquility hovers
in Buddhist halls.
Guqin and flutes
faintly fill the air
with elegant tunes.

From behind
precious tripod cauldron
I watch your gaze.
Fields of dream
paint landscapes
by misty rivers.

Nothingness
replete with sighs
echoes through immortal daze.
A bell reminds
to ponder your fate
in scarlet robes.

Supplications
murmured in trance
veil your face.
When you wake
you are as before
floating yet unmoved.

Now behind the marble pillar
I toss a wolfberry
aimed at you.
Your sudden smile
betrays a soul
east of nirvana still.

Toss it back,
toss it back . . .

Some Observations in a Coffee Shop in Suzhou

In a cozy café in Suzhou
one can browse "The New Yorker" and Doris Day.
(Both old, incidentally.)
Greece on the wall,
America on the table cloth,
Russia on the liquor list,
Hungary on the phonograph,
and a whole territory on your plate.

You put Mukherjee aside
to watch the trash man drop it all outside.
99% of those on motorbikes are female,
plus one male with a boy.

They light an oil lamp for you,
to illuminate your continental breakfast
and your Darjeeling tea.

How many worries you have swallowed so far!
The shop owner lectures you on sugar versus Splenda.
You choose headache over hypoglycemia.

The printed table cloths tell humble stories
of Midwestern proprieties.
None of them is your story,
not even the one entitled "All things grow with love."

Some grow without love.
And some in spite of love.
Like you.

Suspended between clocks and visions,
you know what is out there.
Hanshan Temple.
Red incense burning over grey skies.
Imaginary tranquility
of the kind life does not grant often anymore.

The sugar twirls in your hot tea.
What has not settled by now,
will not settle.
What has been done,
cannot be undone.

the thought: he disappeared

there was a thought
who thought
—as some thoughts like to do—
he would be free
to roam on milky streets.
but he flew so fast,
he crashed into the lamp near the factory,
and bruised as he was,
he landed on your upturned collar,
thinking
—now a habit already, it seems—
that this collar, turned up thus,
is a wall to fortress his demise.
"i love you", he whispered,
or maybe he said, "i am home."
he almost dropped when you
tripped over a soot black brick.
"hold on to me," he begged.
when you sneezed your winter cold,
he whispered to you, "let's go
to the early bakery, just me and you,"
to warmth, comfort, and more.
you carelessly turned down
your collar,
and the thought: he disappeared,
unthought-of, i fear!

lotus

you long
for the moon
and the cool rays
of pallid blue
to soothe silken skin
of pastel hue
to illume this pale purple
and open to the night
in the black green mirror
where silence might
move and shatter
all that is bright
and solid
and to roam in the haze
of midnight delight.

The Y Not Taken

Ay, you ask and question me:
How they rhyme:
A tyger's eye and
stripe studded symmetry?

If you refuse an askance slant,
perhaps elocution matters;
for in 1794's tyme,
was the world of the same cant?

Or did he fearfully de-symmetryze?
In came the ancient tyger,
when the tiger long since
had materyalyzed?

Is there symbol, is there mystery
in the great Y personality?
Was there a question to be posed?
Or was it symply a stylysh hoax?

Or is the loftiest of beauty
not in question or reply,
not in rhyme or in his eye,
but in byfurcation symmetry?

Homeless

I woke up to a snow-laden sky
turned without my watch from green to grey
at the wayside shrine for homeless spirits
where we met on our way to justice

Day follows day into recumbent nights
as we make spirited wicks from plant piths
sitting near the plump cauldron
and staring at insurgent clouds

Our feelings harden like wax in winter
and the heart labours under a coat of frost
Suddenly you look up and smile
the flicker in your eyes so much brighter
than the limp lamplight I remember at my home

BETWEEN PEOPLE

Shadows in Deferment

A Seaside Tree

Trees walk the shore and shoo
the wind away. They shake off the noisy birds
and criss-cross the golden sun. They puncture
the clouds and dip their new fingers into ink
and send green letters into the sand and the sea.
Letters like the ones I used to send to you.
Their branches sweep the air clean
of predictability. The roots hold on to
the young tugging twigs. Far away a storm petrel
drops a cry across the waves. I wish
I could call you that way. When the sun
sets, the trees darken. A cat invades a tree,
quietly. It makes itself light
so as not to disturb the rhythm of the sway.
A shy albatross spreads its plumage
on the lowest branch. Once you spread
yourself over my life. But cats have to prey
on birds. It is in their nature.
The evening symphony rises from the tulips.
A reed harp plays a lullaby. Slowly the trees by the sea
settle down for the night. They make peace
with the wind and forgive the birds.
I play my flute to a moon clawed by trees.
I play a silver white melody. I play from home.
And the notes rise into the sky like fog.
And they sink down again like rain.
The sea brings us salt. I shower in its tears
under the tree. I remember when you left:
the trees could not hold on to the moon.
But I could still hold on to your hand.
And I leaned against you:
Like a seaside tree.

A Quiet Life

Today we walked out of our dream
to sit on the brown bench again,
right across the bare white rocks
that soften the sea.
A summer evening
when we are both quiet,
entranced by the colours of the six o'clock sun
that flicker over the ocean,
mesmerized by the inaudible life
that hangs in the air.
When leaves rustle in the breeze
you whisper, "I think it is a poem."
"It came like water, and like wind it goes,"
I whisper back.
Far away, a sail silently glides from east to west.
I look at you and smile.
Our hearts, too, once crossed over
from one shore to another,
docking on stillness,
picking up each other's thoughts
like little sparrows their crumbs.
Between the waves,
words become slower.
We deny ourselves
the clamour of theories.
We hide away from
the noise of aesthetics.
We hover in life
like dragonflies.
Our feelers as hushed as hibiscus.
We have not yet used up the real.
We know the coming of death.

Still, we sit on the brown bench,
with the sea and the rocks.
When we are both quiet.

Salaam

Pray that with me then be
A pair of pigeons perched on my feet
And upon you then be
The salaam of heaven and of earth

Song of White Hair

White as the snow,
White as the moon,
our hair will be some day…
This last night
I woke up suddenly,
and felt that you are not mine anymore.

Many times already,
we have parted in this life.
All has been seen and felt,
and there is nothing left to add
to this earthly event.

And so you close your eyes,
as we did night after night.
But now my heart stifles.
And I watch the white moon rise over the lake
until it burns my cheeks.

Still Missing You

When you died
there was still a mass
production of filigree
in the sky

When you died
monkeys still rattled in
over a billion cages
of the heart

When you died
two copper plates still
switched places
behind Calabria hills

When you died
birds still beat
their Vitruvian wings
toward south

When you died
the poltergeist from home
leapt like lightning
into the dark

of my heart screaming
swinging on drenched lamps
twisting images
out of their frames

swaying a sword
to slash me sharply
with the rumour of
"Once in a life"

Since you died
I am a button lost
and the thread
is still twitching

Sudden Theft

The one you have been waiting
for all your life baiting
for first did not come out
and then went another route
Then others came and in jest
said "I am the One! Be blessed!"
Some you believed
and some were not clear
But when finally He was retrieved
you felt a certain stir
Yet you did not recognize Him
year after passing year
Then you finally passed by
the same occasion eye to eye
And when then He left you alone
waiting a life time vexed
seemed so much easier than
waiting from one day to the next
Because like sudden theft:
He came and He left

A Gravedigger in Exile

A gravedigger homeward plods,
wearied from our riotous world,
to plow for what was once so dear,
"Far from the crowd's ignoble strife."*

Conjuring the graveyard bards,
he murmurs of "the knell of parting day,"*
digging with his barebone hands,
imploring purpose into foreign soil.

Some sober wish still lingers in the shell,
as though buried with some qualms.
Stories of Chinese ghost fairies
rise out of flesh and yellow mud.

Here rests longevity, stillness, bliss,
solitude and wonted fire.
He came to burrow not for peace,
but for love's mislaid desire.

What still owes time yet to fulfill
he buries under rugged elms again,
placing stones due in fond array,
as though tending to his father's bones.

At night he whispers to the turtle,
"Nothing to show for a lifetime's love
but an empty shell?
Where can a soul find its own joy?"

---

* Thomas Gray (1716-1771), 'Elegy Written in a Country Churchyard'.

Buried Alive

I went to Wo Hop Chek Cemetery
today and began to dig my own
grave. I said, "Help me!" and you
kindly obliged. We dug all day and
you wanted it deeper for me than
all the others. "Where it is cooler,"
you said. How could I resist such
consideration? I look forward to it!

When we were done, we threw our
spades out. We looked up at the sky
from twelve feet under, and we had no
way out. Now I know, G.B. Shaw
said, "If you have skeletons in the
closet, might as well make them dance."
But how will we get back into our
closet without help from above?

Destiny

The moss on the rock
near the lake banters
with the shallow water.
The rock cries.
The moss muffles its tears.
They talk in different directions,
and they ask the water to recede.
The water takes its order from the moon
who is not bright enough tonight
to fathom destiny.

An Ode to Dulin Figs

The smoothness of touch
mingled with the moisture
of eager yearning
The casing barely harder
Than the sweet balm that veils
The shapely heart
A perfect fengshui
For a questing tongue
When all is done
And everything laid bare
Eyes lovingly meditate on
This hard Dulin core
And ponder with a softened heart
The origins of such delight

God's Intentions

I sang for her under a copper moon,
But the soot-black shadows did not shift.

When she finally held up her pallid hands,
The seer did not discern her autumn maze.

Free will drops its golden triumph,
Yet her deep eyes reflect a will.

Voices have grown out of raindrops,
Drop by drop they gather to a final storm.

Suddenly:
The Event.

"Perhaps only in the unexpected," she says,
"Can we see God's intentions."

Do Not Count Our Days

Everything changed when the
east wind whisked our bodies away. But I
followed your tracks to the sea: to where
white waves tiptoe onto land,
and rocks rest under watery skin.

Read to me from the glass shards
on the beach. Translate for me the cries
white seagulls drop into the deep. But do not
count our days: do not count the sand
that is gathered in those stranded shells.

Since I have known you,
I see everything with you,
and what I hear, I hear through you:
as though everything could change.
Do not count our days.

Loneliness

When branches enwrapped her,
the battle thwarted its might.
When leaves beheld her,
the shore consumed the distance.
"Home" the redwood voice whispers,
"home," where there is no home.
You spread yourself over her skin,
yet lonesome fortresses cannot be pierced
with irises like polished stones of ambiguity.
Shut out from your renegade world,
drawn too late into your desperate mirth,
her tears are the tears of solitude:
soaked dark with love.

Broken in the Morning

The fifth hour wind wakens
sienna leaves for a twilight chat.
The sky applies white dust in layers.
The moon gleams pebble pink.
Insects swarm around their abodes.
Not yet fully coloured,
this day dawns.

The first bird's roll call at 4:30am.
On and on croons Thrasher Brown.
"Wacka, wacka" chimes Flicker North.
And Tufted Titmouse grooms Billy for the run.
Others lasso the sky in migration mirth.

Poplar leaves flit in the morning breeze,
like sparrows after a sudden scare.
   Only one branch bends low.
   Only one branch drips frozen dew.
   Only one branch brushes my cheeks.
   Only one broken branch reminds me of you.

At a Loss

Your army of arguments lines up straight
in battalions of tightened syntactics
equipped with weapons of mass semantics
and remaining at staunch attention

until you give the command
to attack without grammatical rules
and to throw all available expletives
into the battlefield of dialectics

If me doesn't defend myself
It's not the fight's no worth
But my ammunition was left,
And no allies to speak of.

I can only wave the white flag
I lift my hands above my head
I surrender my last words at the gate
And turn myself in-to the prison of silence.

A Cake, a Stew, and a Thousand Smiles

I made a cake. I made it the way you like it.
I added saffron and honey, baked it golden brown.
"It is perfect" you said.
I ran to get plates and forks.
When I got back, you were sleeping.
I touched your shoulder and whispered, "Your cake..."
You sighed and said, "I don't want cake. Let me
dream of lentil stew."

I sat down and cried, but I got up again.
I consulted the recipe book and took out the clay tureen.
I added red lentils and onions and garlic and cumin.
I left out the tomato. I sat down and let it simmer in its
broth.
I waited for it to become tender, stirring in all the rest.
I decorated your plate with lemon wedges.
But you were sitting on the roof, poetry in your
hands.
I reached up like trees reach to the sky.
"Your stew," I whispered.
"I don't want lentil stew. I am longing for soul food."
Your words poured down on me like rain.

I went down and dropped the pot.
The cats came and tiptoed around the steam.
I wiped it off my burning feet.
"Soul food" is from across the ocean, a secret
recipe.
I pour into a dish what I know
cats want: milk
I feed the cake to the neighbourhood children.
They look at me and say, "You have dropped your smile."
"Find it for me," I say, and they rush out for the hunt.

At night I dream that you come down from the roof to go to sleep.
Your steps are light, your slippers wet.
You sit on the edge of the bed and you ask, "Where is my cake?"
I wake from my own tears and from the door that opens when you come down from the roof to clean up my mess.
And later in your sleep you whisper . . .
    "We are star-splitters, we are echo birds."
    "We are souls, enchanted with their wings."
Your breath is not that of a hungry man.
I listen to its rhythm until it feeds me sleep,
and I dream of children
delivering a thousand smiles.

Winter Coat

I lingered and loafed for three seasons long.
Alone with my memories of your precious warmth.
Do you recall?
How I enveloped you against the wind, North and East?
How I captured the snow for you, flake after flake?
Yet you shook them off with careless contempt,
I don't know why.
But I felt unsettled.
And when, at times, you unbuttoned
to let the west wind in,
I felt simply undone.
Now it's November, a Wednesday afternoon.
I know you are cold.
Brother Heater told me the other day,
elated about 34 Far and Height outside.
I long to wrap myself around you again,
cloak you with every fibre of my wool.
I have waited 267 dispossessing days,
collecting dust for you, speck by speck.
But you, when you opened the closet door,
you beat me till I fell to the ground.
"There," you say, "that's better."
"Usable," you say.
Abusable, I feel.
And then, without rhyme or reason,
your merciless hands hung me back to myself.

Simply Kafka: Pinky Swear!

You are a hunger artist in a cage
of convention—
and I watch you starve.
A bug kicking its feet
in very thin air—
and I leave you upside down.

Ah, Great Wall of China!
It surrounds your heart
like a fortress made of papier-mâché.
And I won't blow it down.
Pinky swear!

But you have already become
the emperor in his new clothes—
and I am not in your audience.

Perhaps someday you will ask
"Do you know why I never ate to my fill?"
And I will reply to you,
I will purse my lips and whisper,
"Because you were too afraid of the bill."

Sharpshooting Memories

Your grief triggers my grief,
And it comes in battalions.

They lift you up and carry you
Away from sharpshooting memories.

And they leave me in the trenches,
Because time has made me a spy,

Who always defaults to the oldest wound,
A heart turned toward my Mecca of pain.

I don't know how old my injuries are,
But I have spied for relief at every corner.

And when I became the thief,
You became my casualty.

Between People

I came to you with the soul of an emigrant,
An exile from crossed-over oceans.
After we drank together
And broke our bread to share,
We settled in the sand to rest.
And you found a slender willow stick
To draw out
Your borders in the sand.

Simply Darwish: In the End

Perhaps the end is when a woman is
sinn'd against as much as sinning;
when all causes are exhausted;
when charge and discharge
are balanced against all tides;
when no restoration lies
in store anymore;
when in its shade she senses
the pulse of defeat.
Whether trial or test,
whether tempest or toil,
when we weigh whether
all is like incense to dust,
or like dust to mist,
what claim can be laid to this bounty?
Half care and duty its plight,
half love and faith its light.
She is not a paper, not an idea,
not a poem imprisoned by rhyme.
She is not a land, nor a journey.
She is, in the end,
sinn'd against as much as sinning.
Simply human.

GHOSTS OF A GENERATION

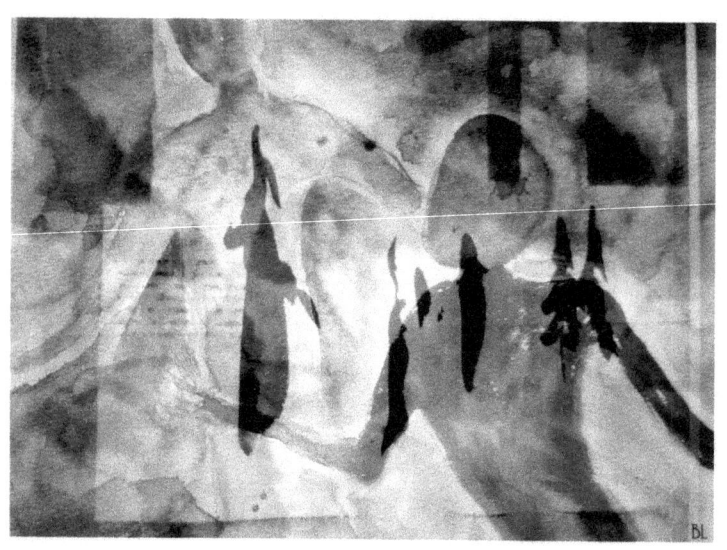

Ghosts of a Generation
A yuefu-themed poem

Sunrise in the south reaches the marble mansion in Cedar Grove. This house has a lovely girl, whose name, they say, is Brocade Grace. "She is skilled with the loom, and picks cotton clouds west of the wall." Her basket is made of cinnamon shoots, its handle, an arch carved of Karnataka wood. When she walks, her raven black hair trails in a tress like curved hanging pods, and her silver bracelets jingle faintly like wind bells from India. Her ears hold twin moon pearls, to brighten her blouse of saffron damask, even her gauze skirt below. When passers-by see Brocade Grace, they drop their loads and stroke their beards. Young men with scrolls forget their scrolls. Young girls' half-lidded eyes cast askance glances toward her. How many springs has this beauty seen, they ask?

    Seventeen springs, but no more to come.

The one she loved rode off on a Celestial Horse, a golden halter on its head. When news of his ruin reached her at daybreak, she walked with slow pace across Fragrant Hall. Stately steps led her down into the river below. Alas, even the crows on the moors paid her no heed! But now, young travellers passing by at dawn wipe their eyes and marvel at the mist spriting on the water. They call her Hovering Grace, and whenever a horse gallops by, they pray for peace. Only the old in Cedar Grove know: every generation creates its own host of ghosts.

Shadows in Deferment

You and I

I left at dusk to return to my home, my ears soon chilled,
winter has arrived.
In the bamboo grove, past the sleepy ponds,
a relentless cold breaks in.
I creak across at the small wooden bridge,
while a thousand leaves sail the mist.
A lonely flurry settles on the tip of a barren gingko branch
while shadowy air sheds faint frost.
The cold straw of birds' nests is deserted and gray,
its touch to my hand as silent and cold as my mother
grave.
Suddenly fairies susurrate of death and rebirth,
and I strain to hear my fate.
Soon they are silenced by the cries of wild geese
from the Old Summer Palace.
Snowflakes assemble in my heart,
while uncanny echoes hush through powdered coppice,
piercing and withered like my father's remains.
Crows bicker and screech.
A blood red sun sets into spider's lacework.
The warmth of summer is long gone,
in a land as far away as passion.
Alone and shivering, but not unfeeling,
I long for a home on this strange winter's day.
My supplication lingers frozen in mid-air.
A hazy half-wit moon lights the path to Scholars Abode.
I rush upstairs, open the door.
Warmth welcomes me, blushes my icy cheeks.
You smile while you eat your Frosted Flakes.
"How was your day? Did you get much done?"
I was bewildered and far, far away.

Obscure things spoke to me of a place I once called home....
"Where have you been, it's only seven?" you say
as you crunch the flakes between your snow white teeth.

The Fancy Maoist Tieniu
at the Monument of the People

I met him on bus #34 in the Imperial City.
He commended me for giving up
my seat to the old chap in rags.
Nice of you to walk me to the Square.
Right across from the Palace Museum.
Your smile almost matches the benign Chairman's,
looking down from the Forbidden City in freshened hues.
Not once did I wish to add my name to a heroic pillar.
Not even next to the Museum of Revolutionary History.
You, on the other hand, started carving
your own name with voracity.
The dead Mao's halo glowing from the Mausoleum behind

   Oh, you cut yourself!
   See the pool of blood budding?

        Trickling
         down
           the
              stairs
                 of
                    the
                        Monument of the People?

Now what?
Your name is not finished.
Two more characters,
fourteen tedious strokes.
While everyone hustles to prepare for National Day,
you must decide:
Preserve your blood or preserve your name.

On the grounds of linear histories,
communist capitalism,
opportune traditions,
mass movements,
and the birth of the "New Wo/Man",
what will you do?
What's the difference?
For you, I don't know.
But I have never been
this curious in my life.

Wounded Soldier

Saturday, 13 April 1982, at 23:35,
on a dimly lit street near Duck Pond Park—
a stout man hobbles
over cobble stones welling grey
like the coal dust from the Jacobi mine.

His gaze fixed yet listless,
he stumbles over his own
shiny brown orthopedic boots,
like a top's last tumbles.
Tenfold his apparition in the rain.

Whether it is Beck's or Jägermeister,
Russian or German captivity,
a denied daughter or a violent son,
loneliness or unbearable guilt,
or the angry wife at home,

I cannot tell
when I bike home from holy church,
the night before Resurrection morn,
and divert my eyes from the shoes
I had polished just yesterday.

At 23:43, behind firmly shut screens,
I shield my war-torn ears with cotton.
But the heart beats its drum roll
and the mind marches on
to the battle front in Hilltop Lane #13.

At 23:59, the doorbell rings into the dark,
its echo soon pierced by porcelain on stony steps.
Gold-rimmed plates, the last of my dowry,
shimmer in shards under the unmoved moon.
On Easter Day, we go to church, and I rise
first, to shine the blood off his shoes.

A Mother-Tongue in Exile

    "Why don't you use your own language
    to write?" the poet asks over lunch.

A mother tongue,
learned in a fatherland,
hurts in this orphan exile.
    I say.
When I try her words,
they dysfunction and trip.

    "Wirklichkeitswund," I quote Celan.
    But you do not understand
    (me. Celan you know).
    Your raised eyebrows—
    the same shape as the stylish silver fork
    on your Imari plate—
    quickly pick up dismay.

"Some people,"
  my mother once said,
"must journey far to know themselves."

But here,
language and identity
undress the heart.
Here,
language and history,
become sleeves

of a remote overcoat.
Between them a shadow
loafs, a shadow, checkered
like winter soot
behind the spoken gates of home.

Hu-Manity

The hu
the man
the human
how to de-fetishize?

Ask Celan!
He buried hu and man
 deepinsnow
until he/she/it melted
in the spring of silence,

Resurrected
 asastone
with one hope:

never to be
hurled again.

White Sparrow

A white sparrow on the snowy sill,
Its voice muffled by ice, by mist
Dark eyes shrill… it claws
Time for being,
For being still.

It came out of a storm,
Casualties still stuck in its beak,
Deserting havoc and loneliness,
To be still.

It cannot summon its name,
It cannot preach or prophesy.
It lost its voice,
Its wings of delight.

Still, I call it
Little Horus, Future Heir,
Blameless Martyr, even
Blood-Red Lover.

I call it Monument of the People;
Cedar of Lebanon; First drop
Of a glacier melting; first flake
Of the Great Avalanche.

Still, still, I call it
Rising Moon, Upright Flame,
And I ask about constellations,
About hemispheres and Heaven,
About words, hopes, prayers even.

I ask about all that I don't know,
The dreams I haven't dreamed,
The places too far for my reach,
About victories and defeats.

Feathers radiate.
Eyes glow like amber diamonds.
It grows monumental,
A Peng bird of the mind.

And suddenly it rises
Into the world again,
To be and be still,

Leaving behind
Havoc and loneliness,
Imprinted on my snowy sill,

Waking me from a dream,
To be, and be still...

An Urban Home

*The city's streets cave in
to memory. High rises
bend toward the past.
Rooms of bliss and remorse float and hover
above the ink blue ocean.
Daily death catches
up with life. And both
winter and melt ...*

One room has dropped anchor.
A stranger wipes the dust off shelves
until he reaches the skin of a ghost.
"Do not joke," the ghost said, hugging.
A ghost whore tells a ghost lore:
Harmony, re-birth, bridging distances.
For whatever begins has already begotten
the end.

Only one bed has the colour of passion—
white clouds of memory float
above shallow shades of satisfaction.
Flattened by experience,
imagination becomes
the new mode of passion.
"Die!" he thinks. But
"die" is not a nice thing to say.
To bend one's head in shame
is also not a new perspective.

It disrupts, sensitizes,
puts the sleeping child between us.
"Leave the city," the sounds
of history have captured us.
It's the raw heart's place.
Do not leave, stay close.
Time's jealous gaze measures
the distance in the urban dark,
and history beats its rhythm
like a giant metro gnome.

*... out of the mysterious city
into a new existence, caved in
by memory. High rises
the moon behind midnight purple
of desire, long life, madness,
imagination, consistency, fortressed
by rooms of reminiscence
that float and hover and tear
by tear fill the urban void.*

Stay with me.
Hold me behind closed doors.
Let your humanity be my home.

Swallows and Spirits

"I am a white-winged swallow,"
soaring forth from the far horizon,
eyes aflame with sweetest fragrance.
She ushers in the Warden of Peace.

He calls on us to open the doors to our hearts,
to pass our days in the Pool of Double Fire.
He opens the doors of Continuings,
but who can find the way?

"I am a violet-green swallow,"
settling wistfully onto the city wall.
Horus guards us from the Boat of the Sun,
Osiris swings his scepter across the Vale.

They call on us to direct our wings
to the branch that blesses the passage of souls.
But our feet are heavy with fetters of humanity,
our eyes used to scanning the night.

"I am a black-capped swallow,"
gliding with ease across the Hallowed Wheat.
But our wings are weighty with our own afflictions,
our eyes blind to the Opener-of-Ways.

Rebellious hearts perish within the reed,
thus the Warden warns.
Fly, fly above your earthly concerns,
do as the swallows do.
But we have no wings to span,
only feet bound to this earth.

When the sun sinks into the far horizon,
we hear the poet chant
his old song of redemption:
"Do not fly, there is no need.
Open the centre of your chests,
and spirits will fly in and out."

A Man from the Walled City

He walks a path in the sun but his shadow is faint,
As though his soul had been summoned
To a place not far, but also not near.
He squatted in a city walled for salt,
Fortified for defense, for triads, for Jesus,
Where fathers hammer on girls' nails,
Yet stones, not girls, cry out in pain.
Where mothers cast anxious looks all day,
Yet boys keep playing the game.
Where bodies are temples of unholy spirits,
Yet incense dims the air of despair.
Perhaps it is not time that has diffused his shadow.
Perhaps it is the prayer ashes that have settled on him.

The Once Red Scholar or June the Third

When the bell tolls twelve,
the scholar carefully ties
his Caponi leather shoes
and rises to return
to his cherry wood writing desk.

Once in black cotton canvas,
he was sent into Northern woods
to be the guardian on the roof,
who at each setting sun fiddled
tunes of blood red ideologies.

Now at the eve of the Incident,
year after year, even decades now,
his wife polishes his black
marching boots until they squeak
to the tunes of left-over theories.

Now in a black chauffeured Cadillac,
he is sent to Northern suburbs
by the guardians on the roof,
who at each Eve of Incident recycle
tunes of blood red ideologies.

Pixie dust and fairy songs,
heretic sermons, Žižek thoughts,
and well-researched papers
sum up the Events in the life
of a once red scholar who,
when the bell tolls twelve,
rises to return
to his cherry wood writing desk.

Cloud Dreams

The bird flies
into white noise.
Its wings heavy
with Gaussian mist.
Its sight paled
by spectral density.
Its hearing masked
by phantom silence.
Its life bleached
Clean.

The bird flies
into white noise.
Its wings heavy
with Gaussian dew.
Its sight paled
by spectral mist.
Its hearing masked
by phantom silence.
Its life bleached
Bleak.

A UN Diplomat in a Hong Kong Jewelry Store

You look at the golden junk in the glass cage
and weigh the price there is to pay.
Your questions rush over my skin and leave
a breeze that shivers me
like conditioned summer air.
You mumble your accent into my ear,
about rights and equities,
securities and values.
Your faint touch charges through my blood,
like the spurts at Bride's Pool.
Your voice hovers in stories
about UNICEF and banks with gold,
like morning mists over Cove Hill.
Your inflection and your fluency
pitter-patter like water in a stony brook.
You talk about the good things you have done,
but I only grasp the clearness
of your convictions.
The straightness of your paths.
The confidence of a meritorious life
lived so far from mine.
How long until I wake
from my wide-eyed slumber?
You pick up a harbour of pearls.
Your teeth smile into a matching white.
We share scores of wars—
Normandy, Nürnberg, Nanjing.
I tremble and you nod,
and your gestures instill peace and security.

And yet I suddenly trip and fall
when you say, "Human rights
are relative." You pay for
the pearl harbour
in the jewelry store.
You walk out self-assured,
while I shiver in your breeze.

just one word

sometimes something escapes from words.
and it disappears. the eye-rain lashes out
like a watercolour painting. they bloom like wine.
they run over our memory hurdle. the paper is already dr
it cannot enwrap our voice. we doubt their meaning.
trees juggle the clouds. animals walk with beady
eyes. cranes shake off their echoes. owls scold
the night. ravens stain our thoughts.
all the words gather around us. it is like salt.
all the trees stand still.
all the animals shed their instincts.
the wall folds up its shadow. but sometimes,
when just one word unearths itself,
everything re-adjusts.

A Portrait in the Old Webbed Attic

In the old webbed attic
Fickle light mixes colours
Lovely and confined
Swelling from within
Breaking out in ultramarine
In the emerald light of Liebfrauenmilch
In the noble white of ground ivory
Images layered, complex, moody
Changeable at the hand of a master alone
Silver lead, red madder, and a hint of massicot
Mixed with linseed oil
Her skin as delicate as a mermaid's
Her black hair seeping night
Her pearl earrings must have dropped
From her oyster grey eyes
When she ran out to the fish market nearby
She shattered first winter ice
With Dutch firestones

The Gods are in a Messy Mood

Today's rain drizzles
with maximum speed
and draws criss-cross patterned curtains
in front of dark green hills
Trees kowtow wildly up and down
seven times seven
and then many more
Leaves swirl frantically to and fro
can't settle onto their own soil
and keep stirring long after being oiled to the ground
(So much water, but no fish in sight
So much havoc, but no monkeys around)
Gravity has lost its quantum mind
Or else the gods
are in a messy mood today
They should get some sleep
and take a break from forgiving
Perhaps then I, too, can rest for a while
from my guilt.

RAVING SOULS

A Raving Soul

Your soul is a wild creature
that does not roam but rave.
It clambers in the brushwood,
thrashes leaves and sticks,
sets fire in flowerbeds,
breaks reeds and bends grass.

It burns forests without a spark,
pours venom out of broken glass.
It twists and twirls without direction,
calls to reason without reply,
until the dark settles into its maze,
where it withers in exhaustion.

It coils like fresh fern under shady firs,
yet still trembles like a twig,
exposed to sudden gusts of air.
Scars have copied onto dreams.
Hypnos is a powerless god.
Nyx douses water on the wound.

Then hours of sweetness arrive.
Arms stretched out like branches,
for shelter and for life.
It rises toward the light.
It settles on meadows of peace.
It fills the air with delight.

A nightjar calls from the forest edge.
Sees the red blood of the fringes.
Looks at the chaos and the dark.
Wipes tears from the sticks
that have struck the heart.

It calls to you without a voice.
It offers sacrifices to tame the beast.
It builds a shelter for his head.
It picks up the flowers that have fallen
and arranges them on our bed.

I step into the woods.
I tread with silent care.
I put a blanket over your shivering body.
I wait unmoving and still—
Lest the nightjar calls again.
Lest your soul should rave again.

A Poet's Demons

we don't know which demon cast
his shadow upon the sleeping poet
the news was brought by a scarecrow
caw-caw, it cried when it perched
coo-coo, the doves of doom echoed

we prepared lentils
   to sustain his body
we brought scented fans
   to douse him in cedar wood
we lit candles
   to shoo away the dark
we hired a nurse
   to lift his head to drink
we summoned ghosts
   of long lost loves
we prayed prayers
   and we sang sacred tunes

we ushered in angels
   to wash his feet
we clothed him in clouds
   to keep him sanctified

but when he woke
   he was shrouded in gloom

we brought in Delilah
   to find out the truth
and thus he woke
   and firmly spoke:

I am the dark owl of the morning star
I am the petrel of the passage afar
I am a bird of prey that preys
on shadows, doubt, on all that strays

you chase the sun, the moon, your fate
then cleanse yourselves from this day's weight
but I will use my heart for tinder
and write my verse into its cinder

Rumi or My Heart is a Vagabond

Rumi is the master of love.
He sent me to you.
He said, "Here is your journey."
And I lost myself on the way.

You never came to look for me.
Because I am not the purest of the pure.
I am not Absence.
I am nowhere near Tebriz.

Because you are too busy searching
For your enlightenment,
Even if it only is in my love.

You look for the palace of the Sultan,
But my love is an overgrown maze.

You search for agates and coral,
But my heart is only flesh.

You wake the troublemaker
And then let him play next to me.

You search for your soul in a sea full of pearls,
And I only offered you crumbs of bread.

You look for eternal pleasure, joy, and life,
Even if it is only in my love.

You grow wings in your heart,
But I am a white sparrow stuck in mud.

Now my heart is a vagabond,
And if you look for it in me today,
You won't see a trace of it.

Go, put your head on your pillow.
Leave me burning.

I am already turning to smoke,
Rising toward the sky.

Toward the sky that was supposed
To expand your heart.

You are beautiful,
Even if only it is in my love.

Go, rest your head on your pillow.
Leave me to my own night.

Gatekeeper

I am the wind that never rests.
I am the shadow that flees across the crescent dunes.
I am a message wafting from the ylang-ylang tree.
I am a dove with silver wings of sorrow.

I am the silence that falls on you like snow.
I am the whisper that dwells in your night.
I am the bliss that tip-toes around your heart.
I am the wine of your fleeting delight.
I am the water that washes your feet.
I am the third eye of your sustenance.

I am the measure for the wingspan of your dreams.
I am the resolve packed compact to fit your heart.
I am the dew that settles on the morning of your hopes.

I am a hunger artist pacing your soul.
I am the golden trumpet of your calamity.
I am the moon that wanes with your desire.
I am the feather that drifts in your loss.
I am your leavened bread of bitterness.
I am the path that lost your way.
I am the home that locked your doors.

I am the sin that subsumes all other sin.
I am the rock that gathers all other rocks.

I am the hour of your humble return.
I am the coal that adorns your crown.

I am the seventh step around your fire.

I am the lonely bird on your rooftop.
I am the pelican of your wilderness.
I am the prison of your solitude.

I am the gatekeeper of your soul.
You are the landlord of my tenderness.

Osmanthus of Despair

You say with some defiant flair
There is no such thing as an
Osmanthus of Despair. But I see
It growing out of your
unpruned hair. It trollopes and it
thackerays and it is not rare. Boundaries
are serrated, and, please admit and be
fair, panicles grow all over your lair.
Two purple drupes mature under the eyes
that seek to dare. Four-lobed tubes sound
a corolla of snare. I wonder if you
could admit to yourself right there
that Osmanthus of Despair are more common—
and on my mother's grave I swear—than
the things that rhyme with 'common pear'.

Hawk of Depression

The hawk emerges and dwells until
It lands on its prey and plumes
It weighs itself into caverns
Constricts sponges
Sinks into the maze
Dulls the beating

It overshadows the breeze
It leisurely moves down
And hovers in a tease
Until it enters swiftly

Into the vortex

That swallows where there is nothing
To swallow
That beats where there is nothing
To beat
That breathes where there is nothing
To breathe

Except when duty calls

Birds and butterflies
Feebly flap their wings
But the hawk's claws return at once
And charge at everything
Just set in opposite motion

Li Yu, Waley, and I

While your dreaming soul
last night was king again,
mine tossed and turned,
unemployed and base.

While you wandered through
the Palace of Delight,
the echo of my steps
found no room to resound.

While you strolled down
grassy garden-ways,
I slipped in the mud
of the muck-pits near my home.

While your chariot glided through
moonlight and blossoming trees,
my car's sprung rhythm is matched
by the exhaust pipe in the trunk.

While you welcomed spring
in royal dreams,
I read your poem
to feel its appeal.

While the faint wind softened
the air of night,
your immeasurable pain
became my immeasurable gain.

Yellow Like Poems, Like Prose

It was yellow,
Yellow like poems, like prose.

And:

Yellow like narcissus
Whose petticoats fly
In a zephyr dance.

Yellow like the sunflower,
The banana, the lemon,

And:

Daffodils,
Dandelions,
Buttercups,
Rapeseed,
Goldenrod.

Yellow like the school bus,
The German post office,
Dutch cheese, egg yolk, corn,

Yellow like canaries,
Like yellow-breasted chats,
Yellowhammers,
Yellow Warblers,
Yellowtails.

Yellow like yellow ochre,
Indian yellow,
Naples yellow,
Cadmium yellow,
Chrome yellow,
Gamboges,
Orpiment.

Yellow like sunsets everywhere

Yellow like the Mayan south.
Yellow like the Chinese Emperor.
Yellow like mourning clothes in ancient Egypt.
Yellow like the tumultuous Turbans.

And:

Yellow like the submarine
That sank deep into my memory.

Yellow like poems, like prose.

What Wittgenstein Said

To rearrange the disarray
of an intangible trinity:

A soul that needs to tumble
like pebbles hurled into a pond
sending up bubbles of relief.

A mind that needs to surge
like swarms of milkweed butterflies
lassooing the skies in March.

A heart that needs to anchor
like a plumb line cast with fierce intent
into the harbouring blue.

To the prince
on the social pea,
to the exile
inside the overcoat,
to the Daedalus of the mind,
the high priest of the soul,
what is asked of you is this:

Do not let me be a shell
tumbled upon its back.
Do not send me a sickle
moon that hooks me still.
Do not hurt
what is deepest in me!

White Flag

A dark kingfishing sky
begs the sea to relent.
Silver morning stars vie for
the light that ruptured in a bent.
And the cold moon mars
wave after wave's fall.
And morning stars
are not present at all.
Fish fly in the flash bow angle bent
of the moon severed by gusts.
You ask me, "Where?"
"Where is home?"
And I, out of the tempest,
raise a white flag,
no matter whence the wind blows.

Black Crows

Black crows screech
and wake me
into morning mirth.

After a first clean glimpse
at the new day
I remember yesterday.

My heart drops.
I pick up stones to throw
at the intruders.

But when I look up,
they are gone.

The rocks weigh
in my hand,
in my heart,

where the birds still screech,
and monkeys of mischief
rattle the cage.

I want to throw them at you.

But what if they ricochet,
and I don't know how
to duck anymore?

Meridians of the Soul

Mysteries of dark passages.
A man lost in its maze.
His heart shape-shifted into a store room
of grey, purple, red and blue.
Eyes that are used to bunkers
never lingered, even when shot.

Perhaps the brown of his eyes
was not formed of soil,
but they caught hers when they
tried to seize the moon.

Though white flags raised high above
the sea of dreams and disappointments
gave blustery directions,
he looked back and offered silence—
an emptiness that roared like a spirit lion
along the traces of lost spices from reed baskets.

There was a time when he captured hearts
with thorns and thistles.
One by one they withered in his flesh.
And there was a time when he swung them in silk scarves.
But now they pulsate on their own,
still listening to his call, from afar
dictating every proud step toward him,
until his call becomes a tutelary guide
to the meridians of the soul.

At Night We Drink

At night we drink
Faces in the neon light
of a city in a rush. We drink
to fill the purple veins
that travel contrary
to all rationality. Reason,
I think you know,
is an animal in a cage.
Yet it rattles no louder than
a moth that flitters
for the flame;
Bauhinias bend their heads
to the spilled milk of the moon:
At night
gravity becomes a beggar.
The distance from blue
to brown and back cracks
and crazes our path. It diffuses
like water in the quiet dark, but it rolls
and roars like storms on a cliff.
Gusts whiplash the skin
we raise like weathered flags.
But a spectral mist
deletes our faces, and our eyes
grow dim under all the lights.
One compound eye
luminesces to woo its prey:
At night
we become beggars for humanity.
And we drink ourselves.

A Swinger of Moods

The course of things is not so straight
Not like the broad horizon
You are, after all, not a spirit level
Nor a taut clothes line stretched to the limit

Sometimes it shoots upward and steep
Like the Matterhorn in the morning
But you are, after all, not the Dubai Tower
Nor the pole holding the line

Sometimes, it sinks and is deep
Like Lake Baikal in July
But you are, after all, not an anchor on a heavy ship
Nor the Earth that undergrounds the pole

Oh, it's rather a tidal wave
In the desert; a Khamasin
In a cave; a crazed glacier
In the midst of an erupting thunderstorm

But you are not a lighthouse
And not a caravan; not a fortress
And not a wild beast; not an ice-breaker
And not a volcano

You are, though, one who can master hurdles
Who can climb trees
And jump off cliffs
Truly, Mr. Frost would say

Truly, one could do worse than be
a swinger of moods

Echo Mountain

Far away Drum Mountain rises reluctantly
against the roll call of thunderous throbs.
Darkly the ridges of Five Tiger Range
march inland from the coast.
Peaks oscillate like maiden eyebrows.
Lines shimmer beyond and above.

The sun's tidy rays lash and rebound.
The sea beats brightness against the rocks.
Warm turbid waters carve grooves at the feet
of flower-strewn hills abandoned to
the yellow-grey waters of Halfmoon Bay.

The sea is covered in leaden armour,
like a giant bird rising up,
its wings propelling the clouds
To drape the sun in floating folds

of mist
that hangs from blue-tiled roofs;
that swallows purple callicarpa blooms;
that throws a shade over the world,
until things swell one into another
under the skies of one hundred seasons of
wars, resistance, revolution, loss, and servitude.

IN THIS WORLD

Simply Darwish: Black Rain Storm

The sky suddenly wreaks havoc upon us,
pours down clear from blackened clouds,
flooding the heart's lingering drought.

The outside torrents rap the bus window,
matching my wild heart beating your name.
I take a volume of Darwish out to read.

The golden street lights after dusk
flashlight the window one by one,
crystal glow worms inch down my page.

Perhaps the couple seeking shelter has
a love small and poor, made wet by passing rain;
or one so strong and rich, it expands the sky.

Now the heavens are grey and blue and orange,
Like cedar forests burning in the distance,
devised by a brilliant craftsman.

Black scraps of cloud criss-cross the sky
like skinny wolves charging at the milky moon,
suddenly stabbed by a sharp lightning sword.

I wade home through water and mud,
past brand new cascades dashing down.
Water always binds me to your name.

I walk behind a singing soul diffusing
into darkened mystery. A world unfolds
like none before. But Darwish whispers calmly:

A simple black rain storm,
no more and no less.

Simply Darwish: Common Humanity

You don't want to be one
Who puts up fences.

"I believe," you say,
"In our common humanity."

I believe in a land without borders,
and in no ordinary death, but

When life's curfew is up before its time,
all grave sites become occupied,

Just like our countries, where
love has become a collective disorder,

Where we have the freedom to die
from burning homelessness.

Where we become shadows on which
martyrs imprint their resolve.

Where we are all blinded, so that
wounds would be felt as scars.

"Good fences make good neighbours,"
an American poet once said.

But not between a land of chronic exile
and another robbed of its immortal claim,

Where grey uniformed soldiers
are ghosts besieging ghosts, where we

Ambush our common humanity,
its future unidentified in the ashes of war,

Where the flesh of the burnt and the unburnt
unite for unmakeable love.

"I believe," you say,
"In our common humanity."

I believe in a land without borders,
and in no ordinary death.

And still you don't want to be one
Who puts up fences.

Peace

Going about as a talebearer
in your discipline of delusions

You are near to their lips
but far from their hearts.
Peace, peace, they shout.
But there is no peace.

If you fall in a land of peace,
how will you do in the thickets of Jordan?

They have sown wheat,
but reaped only thorns.
Peace, peace, they cry.
But there is no peace.

A scorching wind blows from the
bare heights in the wilderness,
not to winnow, and not to cleanse,
but to extract the precious from the chaff

The snow of this country
has forsaken the rock of goodwill.
Peace, peace, they cry.
But there is no peace.

Where shall we go?
Those destined for sword,
To the sword.
Those destined for captivity,
to captivity.

Peace, peace, they cry.
But there is no peace.

The People's Daily

Islamic scholars sweat the Woz contest,
while farmer Li from Jilin walks
The Long March by himself
at a total cost of 16,000 yuan.
Guan Hu is embarrassed about "Come on, Let's Go",
Zheng Dasheng is a crowny for "The Death of Wang Bo".
All the while white ants devour wooden Xi'an.
The Shaolin Warriors applaud the Merchant of Venice,
and Blueberry Morning made its debut
at the Kempinski Supermarket in Beijing.
When I put down the newspaper,
I stare at the broken coffee percolator
that has decked my shelf for almost three years.
And I wonder what news
doesn't make it into my world.

Spies of Sorrow Come in Battalions

An early sun creeps down the hills like a thief,
quells like vermillion on soaked Waterford,
and descends like blood down terraces of rice.

When it dyes the icy sheet on the pond nearby,
a host of starlings change their beaks to red, and
yellow-headed blackbirds echo metallic sounds.

Your vast field of unharvested gold—
yesterday eulogized by brown thrasher choirs—
today is cloaked in mist and morning mystery.

When you turn your back, your heart is as restless
as a thousand chimney swifts in a brewing storm,
and images fly in the bell-beat of their wings.

When you sharpen your ears, magpies mimic bugle horns.
And when your eyes pierce through the fog,
each ear of grain is a cartridge of ripened bullets.

You turn in fear of what harvest it might yield,
and you walk away from what is rightfully yours,
with every step dodging sharpshooting memories.

Actuality

The man, like bread, like water
Like love, like God
Elementary
This man, he lies
Dying
He dies
Lies in his grave
Buried
Only his watch still ticking
Like a stuck echo

Like an echo stuck
In actuality

Simply Kafka: The Rope

It was God.
Was it not?
Who stretched a rope
of sands above this ground.

He had practiced
on the horizon,
and then suspended
a divine line
along our petty path.

Like a needle
in search of a string.
Like a cage
in search of a bird.

We tiptoe along
in torsional distress,
until a giggle reverberates:
two angels whisper behind white wings,

"Is it designed?
To keep balance?
Or to trip the whole lot?
It was God.
Was it not?"

First Day of Winter

The first day of winter
Is inaugurated by a flurry
of a million dancing stars
loosening their white fluffy skirts

Writing After Dinner in Tamil Nadu

In a raven black night,
Thoughts parachute,
One after another,
Remain in flight,
Have not hit paper yet.
Fingers unemployed,
Stained with royal blue
Ink of expectation.
What lands on taste buds
From a faraway subcontinent—
    Betel nut in rusty red
    Fennel seed as green as sap
    Jintan twinkling silver
    Anise pearls crunchy to the bite
    Sugar-boiled into Golden Mukhwas
Traded at Sulekha in the mall—
Settles into sweet saliva,
Like those long-churned thoughts
That finally find
Their landing place
And drop anchor
In a blue sea of words.

To Everycity Turn, Turn, Turn

A man is dirt,
and if you wait long
enough, he will turn
to stone, turn
to brick, turn
to a house that builds
the city and those
who turn back, will turn
to tar, until
the rumble turns
into rubble, and
the bog soldiers turn
up to march in the debris.

How Hong Kong Was Made

Children in the courtyard
Spread barley seeds to grow cities.
But Ah Lee had called the birds
in from the sky.
Only one robin red-breast
was caught in the paw
of the singing cat,
like a wayward butterfly
flickering above its head,
and let go in a twitch
the last of the barley
that grows in the end
into a skyscraper.
Ah Lee was sent to the Pied Piper.
The singing cat still waves its golden paw.
Our children now play
framed by square shadows.
And the robin twitters in its wooden cage.

I Still Think That!

You did not permit me to see
What I did then see:
My own grave
Inside of me
Black, red, grey
The colours of
The process of decay
The flesh in which I walk
Dissolves into dust some day
The masterpiece skeleton
Will turn to white
The ring on my toe
Would clinker silvery
Were it not for the soil
Annihilating my life
Discerning eyes gaze cynically
"You thought you wouldn't?"
I still think that!

Xanthippe

She was chosen
by one born to spite
shoemakers, with a nose
flat like a fish. Unruly brows
and fat lips, perhaps a mirror
of his habit of bluntness,
who knows!

A hunter of dialectics, a
trapper of questions,
he lingered in the agora, talked
to strangers, swam
in a sea of conviviality.
Until his common sense
was imprisoned, alas!

He questioned Laches
and he questioned Nicias
which i know from de Botton.
A certain Meno held unsound
ideas, too. Question,
question and examine
your beliefs,
and who knows!

She bore him three sons,
and she stood to watch
as he drank to die
for his logical demise.
Her foul temper,
did it develop before
or after the hemlock cup?
And who knows?

Life of a Beetle

Back when I was still a beetle,
perhaps because of the dump we lived in,
I didn't think much about such things as
Career, money, love, or any gods.
I got used to not thinking
even about the next meal.
Somehow someone was always there to eat.

But now that I walk and talk,
the next meal always seems far off.
And almost daily someone says, "What will you do?"
"Where will you go?"
I don't know.
What if I just don't know?
All I know is that six legs
were easier to manage than two,
especially if the meals come to you!

A Progressive Ant

The crazed red ant
carries the torch of liberty
through the locked-up wind
that rages within its cage
and through the purple rain
that hesitated too long
and had to join forces with salt.
It scurries up the table of obesity,
a deserted island
full of canned desire.
The smell of the open fish
is only a feeble echo
of the ocean of long-ago.
The crazed red ant
invades the country of fish
and drowns the torch of liberty
in the red sea of preservatives.

Narrow Minded

His mind rented a room
in a small, small world.
In the mirror, the hairline recedes
from the forehead.

The curtain folds like parched flesh
in front of the freckled window.
The world pushes in with drafts,
hankering for a passionate dawn.

Outside, peddlers offer their goods:
Jacob's ladder, Sheeba's gems, idols,
Nirvana, blood, maps, doves, philosophy
yes, even the world.

No need, he says, no room for that.
And he sits and unfolds the napkin
for the meal he eats every day
while travelling the world in the newspaper.

Retreat

In April at the Mongol retreat
snow bleaches the gravel road
and the desert wind weaves its ochre lines.
With knitted brows he points
his camel through Needle's Ear,
hoping to mend his ways
in a hermitage up north.
But when on rare occasion
mandarin ducks lose their way
and invade his longtime solitude,
and he lifts his hands to his eyes
to follow their flight,
the belt of his overcoat comes undone,
shows the tattered silk of his deel,
and his life unravels in distant echoes,
like a spindle dropped,
but still unspooling
fantastic yarns;
like a storm long passed,
but still cresting
runaway desert dunes.
"April is the cruelest month," breeding
sand and snow, and letting long lost
thoughts grow back into the heart.

Nachtraeglichkeit

(Poets after the Cultural Revolution)

Leftovers of love
Like crumbs of brokenness
Strewn in the wood
On the way
They almost mould over
We gleaned them
And between the lines
We turned in circles
There was no witch, no oven
There was a magician, a melting furnace
where all sacrificed home-worn pots
And chopsticks drummed on orphaned lids
Their beats pelting into the Valley of Echoes
Tinny, the heart is steeled for decades
Stroke by stroke patterns emerge
From the netherworld of concealment
Misty like the ancient forests
There was no witch, and there was no oven
But the fatherhoodland gave birth to a step-mother
tongue and children dispersed
Like winter salt and followed the seducer
Those whistled away by the red piper
Marched ahead to clear tunes
But those who wanted to read the writing on the wall
Were whisked away by the Earlking
And they left behind signs of most nebulous style
And you, you escaped

Still and again
They ask you about the mist
While you still search for the crumbs
Of brokenness, and so often now
You find life
Slipped into deferment.

Fairy Whispers

"Ah," the fairies whisper in the underbrush,
"the moon has drawn them like the sea.
Their steps so light and leisurely,
their hearts heavy in sweet delight.
When eye meets eye, the universe shrinks.
The fragrance of flowers in bloom hovers
like mists of providence.
Evenings gray and blue settle like morning dew.
Cracks in the sky sparkle next
to crumbs from a heavenly meal.
Silence settles into silence,
and ghosts of generations
rise in ritual dance.
When four feet part,
the air twirls,
the birds chirp,
even the snail lifts its eyes.
They sleepwalk back into life,
and the Spirit tiptoes around them
like a tender cat in play."

PLACES

India

Sweet anise seed from Madurai,
its taste a sudden surge of exultation,
like milkweed butterflies in March.
India, my Imagination!
On a mid-summer's eve
I dance under a copper moon,
from Megapod to Tillangchong.
My feet touch the ground
like a fairy in flight.
Long dormant desires kindle
to the bliss of sheet lightning.
Half-lidded gazes hallow
nippled roofs of devotion.
I chase your ghosts
and your swift sand serpents.
At 3am, I watch the turtles dance
at the Bay of Bengal,
all the way to Nicobar's Isles!
Even when moody winds shake
sweetness out of summer,
and coconuts drop
on bronze coloured soil,
joss stick, saffron, and anise seed bewitch
the one from prosperity's plains.
With a mouthful of Pimpinella
and eyes closed to your bad dreams
I whisper,
India, my love!

Day of the Strange Tide

Bulbuls in olive green uniform parade
on black branched mangrove trees.
Their glittering eyes dart south to
jaded Nicobar flotsams in the Bengali Bay.

One morning, under a milky sky
tides swell to incendiary heights,
tips of a thousand water tongues lap
where house shoulders house.

The sea's resolve rises yet,
grants the long stranded freighter
a new re-launch in a bowl
that bulges like a fresh blister.

Scrubfowls mewl and swoop
in a lead-blue malignant gleam.
Ruffled like pale picotees,
they flit over mad yellow foam.

When no white sail mars the horizon,
no shrimp farmer harvests the beach,
gods scurry off over pebble-dashed paths
soon rubbled with jetsam lacquered in black.

Never will I swim here again,
or echo the cuckoo-dove's coo-coo-roo.
As the great sea waves with indifference,
children skip over my unseen grave.

Morning Has Broken

At the southernmost tip of the Isle
of Formosa I plunge
into the crystal sea.
Flying fish flash silver greetings.
Swift, frequent, and curious
they jump in swarms
to snapshot the world.
But I dive deep down
to pursue my own dreams;
to envision treasures, sunken
dinghies and merdragons,
precious corals and golden reefs,
pirates and dainties,
and palaces guarded by sphinxes and imps.
When the Prince of Tides
lifts my salty body aloft,
a ruby sun shimmers brilliantly
on silver-red flurries.
When I breathe again,
the wind, too, rises softly.
White sand assembles in dunes
toward the blushing sky.
Doves and gulls polish their wings.
The egret cries "rick-rack, rick-rack"
to summon us all
to the great commencement
of a brand new day.

northern moor

foxes leave the woods through the early mist. birds abandon their nests before dark. the hedge tiptoes along the path, dropping red berries along the way. a thin skin grows over the grass. the moon brightens the memory of snow that hangs on the tips of the trees. he was here, in the midst of change. or perhaps he was the midst of change. i remain silent. my lashes are frozen to the sky. he will come back.

Imperial City

Rain in the Imperial City.
The dust of old scurries over fresh pavement.
Yet some things never change.

Thunder fills the air
over palaces and hutongs alike.
Yet some things never remain the same.

We have all been to forbidden places.
The ashes of old washed away with tears.

After the rain
we are as before.
Alone.
Without shelter.
As the dust of old settles again.

Rain in the Imperial City
falls on the just and unjust alike.

(But I can still see the past alive
in your eyes.)

Great Wall Cocoon

A deserted cocoon
on the Great Wall
must feel as I did
at the ruins of my house of birth.

The sun shines relentlessly
on bickering women,
begging children,
souvenir voices charming the crowd.

Coal ash settles incessantly
On silenced widows,
vying siblings,
and Catholic bells calling the few.

At the carcass of history and memory I wonder:
does a butterfly ever long
for its cocoon?

Fall in Nancun

Rows of young
weeping willows
sway toward fire
grass. Billowy fog fights
with a brazen sun
for a perspective
on East Mountain Province.

The railways glisten with morning
dew. Cornfields lay robbed
and abandoned. Poplars bow to

the wind

coming from the Yellow Sea.

Gazing herdsmen, lonely
rickshaws, grazing cows and countless
sheep, fledgling winter squash
sprout. All seem to follow

the wind.

Only rows of young
willowy children defiantly dance
against the wind and bite
the fog.
But when a far-away
bell rings for dumpling soup,

the battered wind

rules once again
and resumes to bring fall
to Nancun.

Poughkeepsie Valley

She waits for him near
Poughkeepsie Valley.
Streets are narrow and
bridges carry the wind
over wild rivers of old
to towns of civil behest.
History lives here,
the handmaiden of regret.

Once love seemed of promise,
but now, with so much water
under the bridges,
the steady flow of life
has carved out the heart.

The pitter-patter of the brooks
resounds within her thoughts.
What once was a force,
is now but a shallow retreat.

Tartan

Light crimson clouds framed with golden iridescence
Send hue tidings onto winter cotton blooms
cerulean the heavens above, gleaming the earth below
And in between melancholy travellers
Scuffling in the tempestuous sea of words and deeds
Black our inescapable world, white our knitted dreams
Thus sinks the willful Lord of Flare over Poughkeepsie county
And thus he rises to the fair waning moon

Over Nebraska

Snow feathers its wings toward east
Swans plume above lightning sheets
and exhale your blood red breath

toward a horizon that suspends
between a blue metallic vault and
ice snakes that coil around grey hills.

That there is life below, I know
not from the dim lights of distant homes,
but from the sorrows in my heart.

Askance Glance Over New England

An illusion of eternal mountains
Bleached white in ceaseless nothingness.
The lights that flicker and flare
Far above our solid world
Are unfathomable to the spiritless mind:

Askance glances
From the impatient gods
For us fools of the Red Dust.

Ruhrpott Song

Birch of the flood bed
On the banks of the Ruhr River

A raven screeches on its swaying branch,
Has turned me sad

His song like the song
Of the coal mining Turks—

When he screeches his prophecies
You can forget Rebroff the Bearded

And when he sings!—who was Heintje
That young blond Dutch boy anyway?

In Mülheim, Duisburg, Essen
And in Oberhausen, I swear

I'm in love, far gone,
With someone who wears a gown of golden thread.

Wrong! He wears the crown of coal
Of the black soot halo under my eyes.

Through him, in a rush of cadmium
And musk, beauty falls
Into disarray.

Splendour of Visayas

Sun-bleached dry corals
Like giant snowflakes of the sea
Litter the white beach
The wind plays a dry chime
Aquamarine green and turquoise blue
Make the whole sea look like spilled ink
The parrot fish flashes elegantly
The bird in the cicada tree twits its tune
Until the sun summons the clouds
And the waves reach up to catch them

In the Bamboo Grove

Last night the nature fairy lost her way
in the purple bamboo grove.
At dawn, only traces prove her wit:
Radiant snow lingers on golden morning rocks,
vulnerable ice clinks on the almost barren ponds,
precocious frost crawls over withered lotus leaves.
Yet the bewitching air dwells cozy again.
Supercilious greens boldly refuse to bend.
I looked for her behind every strutting tree,
but all I could find was my own reckless heart,
lost in the brushwood of uncertainty,
staring at the morning moon
who teaches me how to give birth
to myself slowly.

New Year in Dougou Village

The stone boat on dragon pond
absorbs the rays with greed,
sways with the eastern wind.
Dry cotton leaves dance to and fro.
Cracks and ripped fishing nets
spin tall tales of bygone days.
But the new red lunar dragon,
ready to charge into blue Anhui skies,
speaks of today's luck,
and of the comfort of hope
for another year in peace.

Only miles down the road,
Qu Yuan once battled his fate.
Had he lived here in nowhere land,
he would not have drowned himself.
For dragon pond is shallow,
and life can be as simple as that.

IN SHORT

The Habit of Turning Into a Shadow

The solitude became a habit
The habit became a man
And it crusted him
Into a shadow

Simply Kafka: The Cage

Mother says:
She was born
around dinner time.
Father says:
It was around lunch.
The truth is:
I was born
Hungry.
But when I eat their food,
My cage grows too
Tight on me.

Saturday Morning

Snow today.
Yesterday's world

powerless under its cover.

Soft though it is . . .

Love today.
Yesterday's soul

powerless under its spell.

Gentle though it is . . .

it stubbornly fills every space.

You

To me you are
The great unsaid
The great unthought
In the pale region of faith
Intertwining
With forms
And with events
Always re-arranging
Disarray

August Rain in Hong Kong

The rain today can't decide
How to drop on us
Bipolarly disordered
Now like cats, now like dogs
Now like pins, now like needles
And as sensitive as lithium
Highly reactive to the moods
Of clouds and winds

Phone Call

Her speech quiet and slurred
Like a kite spiraling down
It lands like a train wreck
In my heart

Anger

His train
Of thought crashed
Speedily into the wall
Of his logic
And what is left are wreckages
Steaming, burning, still wheeling
And, worst of all:
Useless.

The Rooster

A rooster that could scarcely crow
Sat on my window sill below.
His mistress is his errand fate
And makes him ev'ry morning late.

Bygone

Footprints in fresh advent
Snow
Traceless in mid
morning sun

Your Tenderness

When the wind howls   I shut the window

When the hurricane comes   I find shelter

The gentle breeze   however   always surprises me

leaves me vulnerable   shivering

Just like your tenderness

Comfort

Silence has no lack for words
You said with a fragrant smile
That I hold in my hands
Whenever I feel alien to myself

The Way Things Are

God beat his lute too hard
All the notes fell out of the sky
And the moon dropped to the earth
It rolled down the green hill
And bumped this way and that
And finally it landed
Right in our backyard pool.

Life

Stem end and
Blossom end and
In-between:
The fruit

The Icing on the Cage

These poems tackle the shadow; there is no point denying that there is much in them that hurts. We hurt, if we are prepared to tell the truth about ourselves and the world we live in, but this provides the necessary sympathy for everything we are not (which is, of course, almost everything). Like Mary Oliver, Birgit Linder knows that the heart must be broken in order for it to open broadly into the whole wide world. Otherwise, it readily becomes its own death-trap.

Pain in human nature does find moments of relief in stillness, especially that complex, shifting stillness of non-human nature. Many poems in "Shadows in Deferment" evoke that paradoxical silence from which a sweet healing rises; it is a dynamic stillness that is infinitely expressive:

A summer evening
when we are both quiet,
entranced by the colours of the six o'clock sun
that flicker over the ocean,
mesmerized by the inaudible life
that hangs in the air.
When leaves rustle in the breeze
you whisper, "I think it is a poem."
"It came like water, and like wind it goes,"
I whisper back.
Far away, a sail silently glides from east to
   west.
 ('A Quiet Life')

Such moments recall those lines in Boris Pasternak's "Doctor Zhivago", a novel about a wonderfully lucid poet: "This feeling relieved him for a time of self-reproach, of dissatisfaction with himself, of the sense of his own nothingness." All kinds of flickers and shimmers and rustlings find their way into the poet's generally hushed language where we can share them. Like the quiet of the landscape, this un-noisiness hangs on nuances, on subtle shifts in the surroundings, and it leans towards intimacy: it builds an unbounded, inclusive space: "I am the silence that falls on you like snow" ('Gatekeeper').

The blanketing blankness that is a quiet and an openness and an intimacy is found throughout "Shadows": it appears in many guises—it is ice, milk, "the noble white of ground ivory", snowflakes, clouds, sheets and pillows, ghosts, bones, unfurled sails, sand, cotton, feathers . . . The white sparrow in the poem of the same name is "Little Horus, Future Heir, Blameless Martyr, even Blood-Red Lover"—that is: mystery, the people to come, willing self-sacrifice, erotic love. It is also a contradictory space, depending on mood. From the spaciousness of the immeasurable, the same silent nothingness can collapse us into captivity. White, Linder reminds us, is also the colour of submission, of despair:

> I can only wave the white flag
> I lift my hands above my head
> I surrender my last words at the gate
> And turn myself in-to the prison of silence.
>
> ('At a Loss')

Silence sometimes turns its face away from us, and then we can only know that negative side of emptiness, filled with apathy, misery, sterility, futility, living death. Linder knows this side well: "I went to Wo Hop Chek Cemetery / today and began to dig my own / grave. I said, 'Help me!' and you /

kindly obliged" ('Buried Alive'). But poetry exists precisely to call us out of that place, even as it acknowledges its existence. Linder's poetry bristles with detail that rekindles an interest in the texture of all our living:

> When all is done
> And everything laid bare
> Eyes lovingly meditate on
> This hard Dulin core
> And ponder with a softened heart
> The origins of such delight
> ('An Ode to Dulin Figs')

For this reason, travel is an important element in these poems, the atmospheres and particulars of which derive from sites all over the globe, including Germany, America, mainland China, Hong Kong, India. By moving through the world in this way—a way that requires courage and endless resourcefulness—one can rediscover the vivacity of the living texture of things so often dulled by the force of habit and mind-numbing routine. Many of the poems in this collection report such discoveries in places many of us will never manage to get to on our own.

In "The Longest Journey", E. M Forster writes of, "the union of shadow and adamant that men call poetry". At her best, Linder is able to realize this impossible pairing, endowing the unbearable lightness of words with enduring diamond force.

Simon Patton
Kowloon 2013

Defamiliarising our daily bread

Birgit Linder's "Shadows in Deferment" conveys tremendous range in the service of a poetic intention which, across an impressive body of work, holds her reader fast. How? Because the best of her poems allow the reader to breathe, providing a means of egress which makes every successful piece a kind of passage out. And, then, once we're out, we want to return, to turn around and head back to ourselves again and to the book in hand. Achieving this kind of transport in a poem—from poem to poem, across an entire collection—is not easy and, in Linder's particular case, is distinguished by a laudable commitment to craft.

The truism is that the world has grown smaller, but for those poets whose parents, dead or living, have dwelled long afar the world can still seem vast and cavernous enough in the absence of a home. Spaces of long and capacious memory separate them from their own family history. As in the gentle (and all the more poignant) elegy in 'Mother' (who died, presumably, giving birth) or the search for a now-departed father's memory:

> I reach for my father's weary feet
> that have come in from the dusty road,
> like every night,
> to wash his tiredness away.
> Water washes away guilt.
> But his chair is empty.
> The pillow has fallen
> onto the exhausted rug.
> Water is a carpet to the faithful.
> ('Water At Night')

Linder's sensibility is in this way both personal and universal—everyone shall lose, and must lose, his or her parent(s), even as that moment imposes a devastating torque between potent particularity and obvious banality. The loss of one's parent is unique everywhere and nowhere. The best poetry brings both kinds of cut to the quick, as does Linder's here.

The poet also capably unifies several voices to the purpose of the present task. That she can write in several languages allows her to mint interstitial marvels as far as the encoding of experience using brittle letters permits. Linder's is (quoting the title of another poem), "A Mother-Tongue in Exile". For example, there is true translational virtuosity in 'Schatten/Shadow/影子', whereby three distinct columns of text (in German, English, and Chinese) first engage then collapse into (the rewriting of) each other—initially troubling the eye, then instantiating what the mind well knows beyond the eye's tyranny and the cage of the printed page: that linguistic domains may appear discretely on paper, but their commingling in everyday use produces poesis, generates sparks which kindle the tinder of the mind. Broad lexicons at her disposal, Linder's poetry builds fires well; there is a tremendous supply of fuel, indeed more than most, for her to draw from. ...

"Shadows in Deferment" doesn't only inspire the mind's further vision, a precious achievement in itself which promises well for this particular poet's future. Just as necessary, there is a strong commitment to the poetic line—a delicate yet abiding interest in form (including the techniques of rhythm and metre [as in 'I, Too, Sing this Country' and 'Osmanthus of Despair']), as well as a clear appreciation for the energy form can bring to the lyrical voice. (In this, the poet presents a brave riposte to the hegemony of free verse become, one might say, libertine.) Linder dares to rhyme the occasional poem to delightful effect, all the more remarkable and refreshing in that metre is most often misrepresented as a lack of skill or the avoidance of technique:

> One yellow butterfly
> got tired of hiding
> in the fragrant ylang ylang tree.
> She stretched her wings
> and left her sister
> to land on my nose, you see.
> ....
> "I just moved the world!"
> "But, Colias Crocea," I say with dismay,
> "your flapping wings
> have changed nothing for me!"
> "But, Homo Non-So-Sapiens," she replies,
> "You just talked to a butterfly
> from an ylang ylang tree!"
> ('Sister Butterfly')

Linder likewise enjoys the use of alliteration which, at its most effective, helps to establish rhythm and to populate a given line with sound: "Birds are beaded straight on the wire/They gaze into the brewing sky/Dragonflies dangle in the air/Above shadows that fall into feeble forms" ('An Evening at the Ocean'). Such use of formal technique, here bracing, is too often mistaken as evidence of the journeyman poet; far too few critics recognize its subtlety as evidence of mastery.

And masters of form oftentimes scry in homage to their teachers, as does Linder in 'The Y Not Taken', a playful meditation upon the famous "eye/symmetry" off-rhyme in the first and final stanzas of William Blake's 'The Tyger'. Or, again, there is a very nice tip of the hat to Thomas Gray in 'A Gravedigger in Exile', whose appearance gratified me for several reasons, not least of which was that I am clearly wrong in having suspected that I am the only one in Hong Kong still interested in reading his 'Elegy'. (There's a nice nod to Keats in 'White Sparrow', too.) It's best when poets know of the canon before wishing to depart from it; and Linder clearly knows her defining tradition well, before turning to face the doorway leading her outside and into the bracing air beyond. Traditions define here but they do not confine.

Apart from its formal interests, there is also good range toward the cosmological in the collection, as in 'Man on the Moon' which might have been nostalgic but succeeds in invoking scope without an unearned grandiloquence: "When she yelled, / Maria Callas sang to us." The moon-shot and landing are, conventionally, a good backdrop for documenting the family ruptures of childhood. Linder does better than that, by invoking the bluish glow of the grainy telecast and its clicking audio (solar flares no doubt interfering) on behalf of Callas and not the other way around. The poem conveys telescopic space admirably via inverse, with the reader peering through the big end at our sublunar reality collapsed to the point our childhood reckoning admits and, strangely, finding infinity there. The white noise of cosmology emits through the fuzzy perception—idiosyncratic remembrance—of the 1969 event at a time when our minds were first warming up.

And like all strong poetry collections penned by globally inclined thinkers, from Elizabeth Bishop to Tammy Ho Lai-Ming, localities in "Shadows in Deferment" deliver the world most effectively: Cedar Creek, Dordogne, Taipo, Suzhou. In individual poems, even the entire world is never too heavy, and Linder's confidence can delight as in 'Some Observations in a Coffee Shop in Suzhou':

> America on the table cloth,
> Russia on the liquor list,
> Hungary on the phonogram,
> and a whole territory on your plate.

The world can appear such, should appear such, via the refraction of local sensibilities that can, that should, disarm us with their novelty even—or especially—when the whole territory has been staring back at us from the plate for quite a long while. We haven't stared back: we have been too distracted, otherwise, to pay sufficient attention. This is the poet's best task, then, to defamiliarise our daily bread and to transform it into fare to be treasured, as if eating for the very first time. By imparting blessed reminders of the novelty of being, Linder's best poetry reminds us that we have been ourselves responsible for making ourselves stupid by being bored.

Elsewhere, how poets can or cannot handle the moving parts in a picture, the relation of different constituent elements in support of a specific effect or ensemble of effects, separates the merely intuitive, one-shot-wonder-poet from the creator of a body of poetry that lasts. That Linder intends her work to last, that she takes some laudable measure of her poetry's worth, is indicated by the following lines from 'A Seaside Tree':

> When the sun
> sets, the trees darken. A cat invades a tree,
> quietly. It makes itself light
> so as not to disturb the rhythm of the sway.
> A shy albatross spreads its plumage
> on the lowest branch. Once you spread
> yourself over my life. But cats have to prey
> on birds. It is in their nature.
> ....
> I remember when you left:
> the trees could not hold on to the moon.
> But I could still hold on to your hand.
> And I leaned against you:
> Like a seaside tree.

There is ambition in these lines, as indicated by a complex field of inter-relating objects—the sun, a tree and seaside trees, a cat, an albatross, you, and the persona's "me." There is the hint of imagination's reach, too—no ocean-faring albatross (with a wingspan of up to four meters) is likely to fear Tom the shore-side tabby. Hence, perhaps, the first of the poet's "but"s cited here—which may convey that cats must do as cats must do or, slightly more delicately, that the cat is a fool for taking on a bird—a love—of such weight and stately importance. The poem ends best by ending simply—complexity refined to a single, forlorn simile. ... It succeeds in conveying a perfect idea in relation, an idea suspended—held aloft —by a set of relations. ...

Birgit Linder needs no summa here, as her work and career are, happily, just beginning. I look forward to the next collection even more than I enjoyed this one, which was tremendously. "Shadows in Deferment" was a very fine repast, the best companion conceivable of a solitary morning.

Stuart Christie
Hong Kong, 2013

THE PUBLISHERS

Proverse Hong Kong (PVHK), founded by Gillian and Verner Bickley, is based in Hong Kong with long-term and developing regional and international connections.

We have published novels, novellas, non-fiction (including autobiography and biography, history, memoirs, sport, travel narratives), single-author poetry collections, children's, young teens and academic books. Other interests include diaries, and academic works in the humanities, social sciences, cultural studies, linguistics and education. Some Proverse books have accompanying audio texts. Some are translated into Chinese.

We welcome authors who have a story to tell, wisdom, perceptions or information to convey, a person they want to memorialize, a neglect they want to remedy, a record they want to correct, a strong interest that they want to share, skills they want to teach, and who consciously seek to make a contribution to society in an informative, interesting and well-written way. Proverse works with texts by non-native-speaker writers of English as well as by native English-speaking writers.

The name, "Proverse", combines the words "prose" and "verse" and is pronounced accordingly.

THE INTERNATIONAL PROVERSE PRIZE FOR UNPUBLISHED BOOK-LENGTH FICTION, NON-FICTION OR POETRY

The Proverse Prize, an annual international competition for an unpublished single-author book-length work of fiction, non-fiction, or poetry, the original work of the entrant, submitted in English (translations welcomed) was established in January 2008. It is open to all who are at least eighteen on the date they sign the entry form and without restriction of nationality, residence or citizenship.

Founded by Gillian and Verner Bickley, the objectives of the prize are: to encourage excellence and / or excellence and usefulness in publishable written work in the English Language, which can, in varying degrees, "delight and instruct". Entries are invited from anywhere in the world.

The Prize
1) Publication by Proverse Hong Kong, with
2) Cash prize of HKD10,000 (HKD7.80 = approx. USD1.00)

Extent of the Manuscript: within the range of what is usual for the genre of the work submitted. However, it is advisable that novellas be in the range, 30,000 to 45,000 words; other fiction (e.g. novels, short-story collections) and non-fiction (e.g. autobiographies, biographies, diaries, letters, memoirs, essay collections, etc.) should be in the range, 75,000 to 100,000 words. Poetry collections should be in the range, 5,000 to 25,000 words. Other word-counts and mixed-genre submissions are not ruled out.

Annual Entry Deadlines (subject to confirmation and/or change)

Receipt of Entry Fees / Entry Forms begins	[Variable, no later than] 14 April
Deadline for receipt of Entry Fees / Entry Forms	31 May
Receipt of entered manuscripts begins	1 May
Deadline for receipt of entered manuscripts	30 June

More information, updated from time to time, is available on the Proverse website: proversepublishing.com

THE INTERNATIONAL PROVERSE POETRY PRIZE (SINGLE POEMS)

An annual international Proverse Poetry Prize (for single poems) was established in 2016. The international Proverse Poetry Prize is open to all who are at least eighteen years old whatever their residence, nationality or citizenship.

Single poems, submitted in English, are invited on (a) <u>any subject or theme, chosen by the writer</u> OR (b) <u>on a subject or theme selected by the organisers</u>.

Poems may be in any form, style or genre. Each poem should be no more than 30 lines.

Entries should previously be unpublished in any way (except in the case of unpublished translations into English of the entrant's own work already published in another language, providing the entrant holds the copyright).

Entrants keep their copyright.

In 2016
cash prizes were offered as follows:
1st prize; USD100.00; 2nd prize: USD45.00;
3rd prizes (up to four winners): USD20.00.

If there are enough good entries in any year, an anthology of prize-winners and selected other entries will be published.

In 2016, judging took place at the same time as the judging for the Proverse Prize for unpublished book-length fiction, non-fiction or poetry.

Judges: anonymous (as for the Proverse Prize for an unpublished book-length work).

Max number of entries per person: No maximum.
No poet may win more than one prize.

The above information is for guidance only.
More information, updated from time to time, is available on the Proverse website: proversepublishing.com

POETRY PUBLISHED BY PROVERSE

Those who enjoy **Shadows in Deferment** may also enjoy the following.

Alphabet, by Andrew S Guthrie, 2014.

Astra and Sebastian, by L.W. Illsley. 2011.

Chasing Light, by Patricia Glinton-Meicholas. 2013.

China suite and other poems, by Gillian Bickley. 2009.

For the record and other poems of Hong Kong, by Gillian Bickley. 2003.

Freda Kahlo's Cry and Other Poems, by Laura Solomon, 2015.

Heart to Heart, by Patty Ho, 2010.

Home, away, elsewhere, by Vaughan Rapatahana. 2011.

Immortelle and bhandaaraa poems, by Lelawattee Manoo-Rahming. 2011.

In vitro, by Laura Solomon. 2nd ed., 2014.

Irreverent Poems for Pretentious People, by Henrik Hoeg, 2016.

Life Lines, by Shahilla Shariff, 2012.

Moving house and other poems from Hong Kong, by Gillian Bickley. 2005.

Of Leaves and Ashes, by Patty Ho, 2016.

Of symbols misused by Mary-Jane Newton. March 2011.

Painting the borrowed house: poems, by Kate Rogers. 2008.

Perceptions, by Gillian Bickley. 2012.

Rain on the Pacific Coast, by Elbert Siu Ping Lee, 2013.

refrain, by Jason S. Polley. 2010.

Shadow play, by James Norcliffe. 2012.

Shadows in Deferment, by Birgit Linder. 2013.

Shifting Sands, by Deepa Vanjani, 2016.

Sightings, by Gillian Bickley. 2007.

Smoked pearl: poems of Hong Kong and beyond, by Akin Jeje (Akinsola Olufemi Jeje). 2010.

The Layers Between, by Celia Claase, 2015.

Unlocking, by Mary-Jane Newton, 2014.

Wonder, lust & itchy feet, by Sally Dellow. 2011.

POETRY – CHINESE LANGUAGE

For the record and other poems of Hong Kong, by Gillian Bickley. Translated by Simon Chow. 2010. E-bk.

Moving house and other poems from Hong Kong, translated into chinese, with additional material, by Gillian Bickley. Edited by Tony Ming-Tak Yip. Translated by Tony Yip and others. 2008.

~~~

FIND OUT MORE ABOUT OUR AUTHORS BOOKS AND EVENTS

Visit our website:
http://www.proversepublishing.com

Visit our distributor's website: <www.chineseupress.com>

Follow us on Twitter
Follow news and conversation: twitter.com/Proversebooks>
OR
Copy and paste the following to your browser window and follow the instructions:
https://twitter.com/#!/ProverseBooks

"Like" us on www.facebook.com/ProversePress

Request our free E-Newsletter
Send your request to info@proversepublishing.com.

Availability
Most books are available in Hong Kong and world-wide from our Hong Kong based Distributor,
The Chinese University Press of Hong Kong,
The Chinese University of Hong Kong, Shatin, NT,
Hong Kong SAR, China.
Email: cup-bus@cuhk.edu.hk
Website: <www.chineseupress.com>.

All titles are available from Proverse Hong Kong
http://www.proversepublishing.com

and the Proverse Hong Kong UK-based Distributor.

We have **stock-holding retailers** in Hong Kong,
Singapore (Select Books),
Canada (Elizabeth Campbell Books),
Andorra (Llibreria La Puça, La Llibreria).
Orders can be made from bookshops in the UK and elsewhere.

Ebooks
Most of our titles are available also as Ebooks.

www.ingramcontent.com/pod-product-compliance
Lightning Source LLC
Chambersburg PA
CBHW051127160426
43195CB00014B/2373